Evans Bell

A Letter to Sir James Davidson Gordon ..

Evans Bell

A Letter to Sir James Davidson Gordon ..

ISBN/EAN: 9783744765060

Printed in Europe, USA, Canada, Australia, Japan

Cover: Foto ©ninafisch / pixelio.de

More available books at **www.hansebooks.com**

LETTER

TO

SIR JAMES GORDON, K.C.S.I.

A

LETTER

TO

SIR JAMES DAVIDSON GORDON,

K.C.S.I.,

RESIDENT AT MYSORE,

LATE CHIEF COMMISSIONER FOR THE GOVERNMENT OF THE MYSORE TERRITORIES,

FROM

MAJOR EVANS BELL,

LATE OF THE MADRAS STAFF CORPS,

AUTHOR OF "LAST COUNSELS OF AN UNKNOWN COUNSELLOR", "THE OXUS AND THE INDUS", "RETROSPECTS AND PROSPECTS OF INDIAN POLICY", "THE MYSORE REVERSION", ETC.

LONDON:
CHATTO AND WINDUS, PICCADILLY.

1882.

NOTICE.

This Letter is not written merely for the correction or edification of the gentleman to whom it is addressed, but has, to make use of his own words, "a political purpose". Some words of preliminary explanation are, therefore, necessary to introduce the subject and to make it generally intelligible.

The Maharajah of Mysore, who was placed on the throne in 1799 by the allied Powers, the Honourable East India Company, and the Nizam of Hyderabad, died in March 1868, and in accordance with the decision of Her Majesty's Government, was succeeded by his infant kinsman and adopted son, the present Maharajah.

In a letter dated 7th May 1868, the Commissioner of Mysore appointed Major Charles Elliot, C.B., to the task of rearranging the Palace Establishments, and taking inventories of all the Maharajah's effects and personal property. For the purpose of assisting in this special duty, the services of Mr. C. Rungacharloo, a Deputy Collector, were placed at the disposal of the Commissioner of Mysore by the Government of Madras.*

Major Elliot and Mr. Rungacharloo were occupied for five months in arranging the various Palace Establishments, and placing the personal property of the Maharajah in a condition of order and security.†

* *Papers, Mysore Government,* 385 of 1878, pp. 60, 62.
† *Ibid.,* p. 60.

Mr. Bowring, Chief Commissioner of Mysore, in a despatch to the Government of India, dated 29th of November 1868, says that "the difficult task of examining and cataloguing the Maharajah's property has been performed by Major Elliot and his assistant, Mr. Rungacharloo, with scrupulous care and fidelity, and great credit is due to both these officers for the excellent arrangements made by them to prevent spoliation or loss."*

These officers consequently received the thanks of Government, and Mr. Rungacharloo was appointed Controller of the infant Maharajah's Household.

The most important part of the Palace property was described and valued as follows:—

	RS.
Jewellery	26,02,233
The jewels used by the Rajah's grandson	3,68,920
The gold plate and other gold articles	4,16,570
The silver plate and other silver articles	1,80,571
And gold coins	1,70,316
Total estimated value	37,38,610†

Turning the rupees roughly into English money, we may say that the plate and jewellery found in the Mysore Palace in 1868 amounted in value to about £350,000.

According to the lists and valuation made on this occasion, the goods in the Palace Wardrobe were valued at Rs. 2,77,856, or about £25,000.

And it may be observed that a great proportion of the contents of such a Wardrobe, consisting of gold and silver brocades and tissues, would be almost as durable, and as convertible into cash, as plate or jewellery.

* *Mysore Government*, 385 of 1878, p. 92.   † *Ibid.*, p. 94.

In the course of some judicial proceedings in 1874 it became known as an absolute fact that the Wardrobe property had decreased by about one-sixth, or £4,000, in value, while in the charge of Mr. Rungacharloo, by a series of what were called " burglaries".

About the same time scandalous rumours were current in Mysore as to a considerable diminution in the value of the Jewel-room property having likewise taken place under the Controllership of Mr. Rungacharloo.

These facts and rumours were brought to the notice of the Chief Commissioner of Mysore, Sir Richard Meade, in 1874, and seem to have received very slight attention.

In 1877 the fact of discrepancies and deficiencies in the value of certain articles in the jewel-room, when compared with their value as recorded in the original catalogue of 1868, became accidentally known to the Chief Commissioner, Mr. Saunders, who made no serious investigation, but was contented with a simple reference to Mr. (now Sir James) Gordon, who had acted as Guardian in 1872, and was satisfied with the following official "Note" from that gentleman :—

"I revised and rearranged, and placed in new receptacles designed by myself, the Palace jewels in July 1872, or about that time. The work was done in my presence, in that of Mr. Rungacharloo, the Controller, and all the Palace officials concerned. It was a work much required. It occupied us for several hours daily for more than six weeks. I found several such errors as that under notice, but at this distance of time, and considering the very great number of jewels, and the great number of such inaccuracies, I cannot recall the particulars of the jewels referred to herein—5, 9, 77."

All these incidents, as communicated to me, gave form and colour to the rumours that had prevailed, of some of the State Jewels having been lowered in value by a process of abstraction and substitution.

The terms of Mr. Gordon's "Note" subsequently appeared still more remarkable, when it became known that Colonel G. B. Malleson, for whom Mr. Gordon acted as Guardian in 1872, had, in December 1874, on the authority of Mr. Rungacharloo, and expressly for his exculpation, certified to "the accuracy of the original lists", even to the absence of "a single error".

Under the circumstances mentioned in the following Letter, a Memorandum signed with my initials, calling for an independent inquiry, was published in a Calcutta daily paper, the *Statesman*, on the 7th of April 1880, and republished on the 16th of June in the same year. Mr. Gordon was called upon for an explanation; and wrote an explanatory Memorandum dated the 29th July 1880, which the Government of India declared to be satisfactory.* Mr. Gordon and Mr. Rungacharloo, the two officials most interested—the two men who alone could be held answerable—were called upon to report upon themselves, and they reported favourably. Their explanation, which was promptly published, appeared to me so very unsatisfactory that I at once addressed the Government of India officially,† considering that I should not be warranted, as a loyal citizen, or as a pensioned servant of the public, in withholding such humble aid as lay within my power towards the elucidation of a very grave matter that had been manifestly mismanaged. The following Letter testifies to the failure of my efforts in that direction, and contains, I believe, a full justification of the course that I have taken.

E. B.

* *Mysore Papers*, No. 1 of 1881, pp. 146 to 150.   † Appendix B.

TO

SIR JAMES DAVIDSON GORDON, K.C.S.I.,

RESIDENT AT MYSORE,

Late Chief Commissioner for the Government of the Mysore Territories.

SIR,

In a Memorandum submitted by you to the Viceroy of India in Council, and dated "Government House, Bangalore, the 29th of July 1880", you accuse me of having made "*strange misstatements*". In an Order of the Mysore Government, dated, "Bangalore, the 14th of March 1881", you accuse me, in stronger and more offensive language, of having, "*with the aid of garbled quotations from official correspondence and papers, attempted to weave for a political purpose a malicious story of spoliation and loss of the Mysore State Jewels.*" You charge me with perverting the truth, "garbling" documents, and falsifying evidence, from malicious motives.

Your Memorandum above-mentioned was published after the last Session of Parliament, in a Blue Book.* Your Order and Proceedings of the 14th of March 1881, forming the subject of an appeal to Her Majesty's Government, by B. Ramaswamy Iyengar, against his summary dismissal from the place of Sheristadar to the Mysore Residency, have been printed, and many copies have been distributed here, at the India Office, and in other influential circles.

After eighteen years of labour in the dry soil of

* *Mysore Papers*, No. 1, (C.—3026) 1881.

Indian politics, where not much fame or profit is to be reaped, I cannot allow my small harvest of reputation for truthfulness, fairness, and moderation in controversy, to be scattered and spoiled, or my humble field of usefulness to be trampled and torn up, by means of official slander. I say that you have accused *me* personally of "weaving a malicious story", and of "garbling" documents, because for you, and for everyone interested in Mysore affairs, the Memorandum I published in the Calcutta *Statesman*,* under my initials "E. B.", reprinted in the same Blue Book of last year, and against which your strictures are directed, was not anonymous.

I say, furthermore, that your denunciation of the Memorandum signed "E. B.", in paragraph 15 of your Order dismissing the Residency Sheristadar, as the result of "*a party agitation*", and as "*a mischievous invention set up by his caste-men*", is totally unjustifiable. You knew quite well when you penned or passed that Order that I was the writer of the Memorandum signed "E. B.", and that my information was derived from Colonel Macqueen. You must have been, or ought to have been, well aware that the Sheristadar's "caste-men" could not have had any influence whatever over the decisions of Colonel Macqueen and myself.

The Iyengars of Mysore, you may say—in fact you have said it—are hostile to Mr. Rungacharloo; and the discharged Sheristadar belongs to that clan of Brahmins. I believe you are to some extent right as to the resentment felt and expressed by many Mysoreans of that caste, on account of their being displaced by Mr. Rungacharloo's friends from Madras. There has been plenty about it in the Madras and Mysore newspapers. The Sheristadar, however, is, I am assured, a respectable plodding clerk, quite unconnected with any "party agitation", and he had not, I imagine, anything to complain of, until you most iniquitously deprived him

* 7th of April and 16th of June 1880, *Mysore Papers*, No. 1 of 1881, p. 141.

of his office and his pension, on an unfounded suspicion of divulging your Note of September 5th, 1877. Your suspicion in his case is most certainly groundless, and viewed either from a judicial or an administrative point of view, your proceedings against that poor man, dated the 14th of March 1881, are preposterous. Our information did not come from that quarter. So far as I can understand, the most valuable intelligence placed at my disposal has come from European sources. You are probably not aware of the surprise and disgust very generally felt in the English community of Mysore, at your apparent infatuation regarding Mr. Rungacharloo's merits. The greatest care in testing and verifying the information before us, has been taken by Colonel Macqueen and by myself. What excuse have you for imputing bad motives to him or to me? And how, except through perfect bewilderment, could you impute such an absurd motive to the author of the Memorandum signed "E. B.", as that of advancing the interests, or avenging the wrongs, of the Iyengar Brahmins, the Sheristadar's "caste-men". In such a connection I can attach no other meaning to the terms, "a party agitation", and "a political purpose", which you charge the poor Sheristadar with assisting. I had, indeed, and still have, "a political purpose", and will shortly explain it, but assuredly it had nothing to do with promotions or dismissals of Mysoreans or Madrassees. Placed at the head of Mysore affairs, you can hardly be ignorant of the fact, that I have not had for many years any correspondent in that country. Colonel Macqueen, who has been quite frank with you, and with every other person entitled to know his intentions and objects, informed you long ago, that he had one Native correspondent in Mysore, and one only—a gentleman of distinguished position and reputation, who has always held himself apart from all " caste" rivalries and dissensions, who corresponds with several other retired English officials, and who had no more to do with the steps we have taken than yourself. You were acquainted with Colonel Macqueen, and had corresponded with him. My old friend, as I said before, was perfectly frank with you. You had not followed his advice to avoid the Guardianship. When it became impossible to doubt your determination— contrary, likewise, to his remonstrance—to force Mr. Rungacharloo on the Maharajah, and on the Government of India, as the Minister of Mysore, Colonel Macqueen gave you fair warning that he would do all in his power to oppose your plans, or to expose them. You observed, in one of your letters to him, that you knew my name, and admitted that the initials, "E. B.", concealed no mystery from your eyes. The Memorandum having been written merely to suggest the urgent want of some inquiry and of certain precautions, we considered that while there ought to be no secret about the authorship, the full signature might seem defiant and disrespectful to the Government of India.

Apart from your personal acquaintance and correspondence with Colonel Macqueen, you must, from your access to all the confidential records, have understood his very natural and very legitimate interest in the affairs of Mysore. The intimate and attached friend for many years of General Sir Mark Cubbon, he became convinced—in conformity with the views adopted by that eminent man, slowly, deliberately, almost reluctantly—that the annexation of the Mysore State, as recommended by the authorities at Calcutta, would be, after the Queen's Proclamation of 1858, alike unjust and impolitic. Having retired from the position of Judicial Commissioner, he became associated with Dr. John Campbell, for many years Durbar Surgeon at Mysore, as an advocate with the Home Government for the Maharajah's formal reinstatement. This agency, established with the knowledge and consent of the Viceroy, Lord Lawrence, though he withstood its object, saved the Mysore State from destruction, and the Empire from great discredit. My own small share in that good work of 1866, is one of my most pleasing recollections; but although the Mysore State was rescued from extinction by the adopted heir being recognised, the old Maharajah failed to obtain his personal release from supersession. How very nearly it was obtained—the decision of the Secretary of State being reversed by a vote of the Cabinet—may some day, perhaps, be told. To the aged Prince it would merely have been a restitution of honour. He had agreed to claim no active share in the Government. The documents are extant whereby Colonel Macqueen was to have been placed at the head of the Mysore administration with Colonel Gregory Haines, for many years the right-hand man of Sir Mark Cubbon, in charge of the revenue and finances.

When Sir Mark Cubbon retired in 1861, he left an accumulated surplus in the Mysore treasury of a million sterling. The Rajah's personal restoration being refused, and annexation being at the time confidentially decreed, the creation of new departments, new jobs, and new salaries, went on under successive Chief Commissioners, until it fell to you to hand over his dominions to the young Maharajah in 1881, burdened with a debt of about a million and a half. I will not enter on visions of what might have been if the real successors of Sir Mark Cubbon had been allowed, while the old Rajah was yet living, to restore the simple and economical fabric of a real Native State. The experiment was not to be tried. The costly structure called the Mysore Commission, remained, with little change, during the last years of the minority, and still seems to survive in a form sufficiently strong to overawe and overshadow the young Maharajah, and to crush local interests and opinions. But Colonel Haines, though not recalled to a high administrative post, was chosen by the old Maharajah, and by the Secretary of State, Sir Stafford Northcote, to be Guardian of the infant heir.* Both the Chief Commissioner of Mysore and the Secretaries at Calcutta betrayed at once their conviction that Colonel Haines was too well informed and too much respected at Mysore to be a manageable Guardian,† and the arm of

---

* *Mysore Papers* (385 of 1878), pp. 13 and 19.
† *Ibid.*, pp. 12, and 16, 17.

the Secretary of State was not long enough to reach to Mysore. Nor, in fact, was the arm of the Viceroy.

The most important of all the injunctions on which Her Majesty's Government had insisted, and which was, with equal solemnity, so far as written words went, handed on to the Chief Commissioner of Mysore by the Viceroy in Council, was that "great care should be taken to remove from" the young Maharajah's household "all persons likely to initiate him, at an early age, into the vicious and demoralising practices of the zenana."* The Chief Commissioner of Mysore, being determined not to tolerate a really competent Guardian, such as Colonel Gregory Haines would have been, broke through, and was allowed to break through, the rules prescribed by the Government of India, that the Guardian should appoint the Maharajah's attendants and instructors, and that the Chief Commissioner was not to interfere in details.† Lord Lawrence, who had framed those rules, would hardly have allowed them to be thus instantly set aside, but unfortunately he left India just at this crisis, and the newly installed Viceroy, Lord Mayo, was not yet capable of dealing with Secretaries or with Provincial magnates. Immediately on his arrival, in 1869, Colonel Haines, from remarkable insight and knowledge of persons and usages in Mysore, detected a sinister alliance between Mr. C. Rungacharloo, the Controller of the Household, and a person placed in one of the most important posts in the zenana, named Murree Mullapa, a man of notorious infamy for his "vicious and demoralising practices". Relying on the salutary rules prescribed by the Government of India, Colonel Haines tried to break up this close partnership, but more particularly insisted on the removal of Murree Mullapa, against whose presence in the Palace, under any circumstances, he absolutely protested. That was quite enough; Colonel Haines's remonstrances were condemned as presumptuous, and he was worried out of the place. When Mr. Bowring, then Chief

* *Mysore Papers* (385 of 1878), p. 82.
† *Ibid.*, p. 81.

Commissioner, supported by the Foreign Office at Calcutta, refused to purify the Palace, by removing an obscene parasite, Colonel Haines at once resigned. The hands of Murree Mullapa and Mr. C. Rungacharloo were, of course, much strengthened, and their domination converted into a terror by the failure of Colonel Haines to dislodge them, and his own consequent removal. You have, doubtless, seen the correspondence in February and March 1869, which explains the first Guardian's resignation. From that day the reign of Mr. Rungacharloo commenced. Your responsibility commences at a later period.

I must not speculate on the different spirit and direction that might have been given to the present Maharajah's domestic and political training, if Colonel Gregory Haines had been able to remain for one or two years at Mysore as Guardian. Perhaps the young Hindoo Prince might by this time have been less proficient in polo and lawn tennis, and have seen more of his own people, who, after all, and in spite of the nineteen English coffee planters of whom we have heard so much, are for the most part Hindoos. But these, likewise, are mere visions of what might have been, and I have more prosaic work on hand.

You were fully acquainted, then, with the fact, that I was the author of the Memorandum in the Calcutta *Statesman*, signed "E. B.", and that it was written and published in counsel and concurrence with Colonel Macqueen, with whom you had recently corresponded on Mysore affairs. You charge me with "malice", by which you must mean, I suppose, bad motives of some sort. You also charge me with publishing "a mischievous invention set up by" the dismissed Sheristadar's "caste-men". I defy you to make out anything like malice, either in the moral or the legal sense, in my proceedings.

We now come to your charge of "setting up a mischievous invention". The facts and official papers on which I founded my call for an inquiry—and I have done nothing more—were certainly not my "invention".

Although you talk vaguely of "strange misstatements", and of "garbling documents", you admit the accuracy of all my citations, including your Note of the 5th of September 1877; and with one exception, which soon ceases to exist, you do not impugn one of my statements. You declare, in your Memorandum of the 29th July 1880, that "save in the published Memorandum" signed with my initials, you had "never heard of any loss of jewels from the Mysore Palace"; and that "no one in the Palace is able to conjecture to what the Memorandum refers."* And yet, after a lapse of only four months, in November 1880, you have to admit, with reference to the loss of £300 in the value of a single jewel, that you had "heard" of this "loss", and of several others, in 1872, and that you are "able to conjecture" how the loss occurred. Here are your own words:—"When the lady died, in 1871, the bracelet, found amongst her jewels, was discovered to be of less value—It is believed in the Palace that the relations of the lady substituted an inferior jewel whilst it was in her possession."†

I leave you to reconcile the two statements. I reject your conjecture as to the personality of the felonious agents, but I beg to point out that you testify to the very process which the Memorandum signed "E. B." suggests, loss by "abstraction and substitution", by diminution in value without apparent deficit in the number of articles.

I am really puzzled to know what your actual contention is. I cannot believe you to maintain that until my Memorandum appeared in the *Statesman*, there were no scandalous rumours afloat as to defalcations of value in the Mysore Jewel Department, and that my suggestion of such scandals prevailing in Mysore is "a mischievous invention". You had, by your own account, found good cause for such scandals in 1872. If you, who were Judicial Commissioner in 1874, and had recently acted as Guardian, never heard

---

* *Mysore Papers*, No. 1 of 1881, p. 146.
† *Ibid.*, p. 168.

of the scandalous rumours regarding the jewels that were in circulation in that year, and have been current ever since, until 1880, your ears were less open than those of any other officer in the Mysore Commission.

There is, or was—for I do not know if he is alive—a Brahmin named Kanchi Rungachari, formerly one of Mr. Rungacharloo's hangers-on, who was apprehended at Mysore a few days before the Maharajah's enthronement in March 1881, brought to Bangalore in custody, held to the excessive bail of Rs. 1,000, somewhat hurriedly tried on the charge of defaming Mr. Rungacharloo, and sentenced to a year's imprisonment. Now, the defamatory libel consisted of petitions presented to the Chief Commissioner of Mysore, in 1874, embodying those very scandals regarding the Palace jewels which you, addressing the Government of India on the 29th of July 1880, say you never heard of "save in the Memorandum published in the *Statesman*," under my initials, in April 1880. But you had heard of Kanchi Rungachari before his rather tardy trial and imprisonment in 1881. If I am not very much misinformed, Sir Richard Meade, who was Chief Commissioner in 1874, sent some of this man's petitions in 1874 to you for inquiry and report. I cannot, therefore, understand how in 1880 you had apparently forgotten your official acquaintance in 1874 with these scandalous rumours. I am not, however, in the least surprised at the allegations of this obscure person, even though abetted and guaranteed by Linga Raj Urs, a member of the Rajah's family, having been disregarded. That is quite in conformity with Anglo-Indian official custom in such cases. And although I cannot exactly understand, I can very fairly conjecture why the charge of defamation, pressed on to conviction and sentence in 1881, was not promptly brought against Kanchi Rungachari in 1874. Mr. Rungacharloo had quite enough of prosecuting Kanchi Rungachari, and of otherwise judicially exhibiting himself in that year.

In 1872 and 1873 there were several so-called "burglaries" in the Palace Wardrobe at Mysore, for the charge of which Mr. Rungacharloo was solely responsible, and property to the value of about £4,000 was lost. There is one recurrent peculiarity in the annals of the Mysore Palace Controllership and Guardianship, which appears to have caused hardly any local misgivings, and that is that information of losses and deficiencies in the Palace property has always come to the outside world, and even to the authorities, by some accident or irregularity, and never in due form or by a timely report. For example, the Wardrobe burglary of 1872—which must not be confounded with " the Palace Treasury burglary"*—was not reported to any of the authorities, and only became known, after the lapse of two years, to the Chief Commissioner of Mysore,—as we are told in Sir Richard Meade's Order of November 30th, 1874, and in his letter to the Guardian, Colonel Malleson, dated 11th of January 1875,† from the proceedings in the Magistrate's Court on the occasion to which I am now about to refer.

In September 1874 several prisoners were tried and convicted for one of these " burglaries"—whether the second or third is not quite clear. Kanchi Rungachari, who was one of the witnesses at this trial, stated that Mr. Rungacharloo, the Controller of the Household, had instructed him to induce two men to come forward and confess to the palace " burglary", on a promise of a reward of Rs. 500 for each of them. This deposition conveyed such a foul imputation against Mr. Rungacharloo, that, in order to rebut it, he brought a charge of perjury against the witness, Kanchi Rungachari, who was tried in November 1874 before the Town Magistrate of Mysore—*and acquitted*. The Magistrate considered it clear enough that Mr. Rungacharloo had, in fact, privately offered a reward of Rs. 500 in this matter; and he narrowed the issue to two alternatives: (1) the reward was either offered for the production of Queen's evidence ; or (2) it was offered to suborn false

---

* *Mysore Papers*, No. 1 of 1881, p. 173. I confess I know nothing of this burglary, except that it is quite distinct from the Wardrobe " burglaries".

† Appendix A.

witnesses. He decided for the former and more favourable supposition, and dismissed the defendant with some rather contemptuous remarks regarding the prosecutor.

It can easily be conceived that, after the failure of this prosecution for perjury, Mr. Rungacharloo may not have considered it prudent or politic to open the floodgates of public debate by indicting his former dependant for defamation. At any rate, Kanchi Rungachari was left to his own devices until March 1881, in the last days of your Chief Commissionership, and just before the administration of Mysore was transferred to Mr. Rungacharloo, so that the defamatory petitioner was safely lodged in gaol, after seven years' immunity, by the authority of a British officer.

This unsuccessful prosecution for perjury, and the long series of civil suits brought by the widow of Murree Mullapa, not settled until 1879, by no means exhaust the list of Mr. Rungacharloo's appearances in the Mysore courts of justice in 1874. He was in that year defendant in two cases of trespass and assault brought against him by the widow of Devaraj Urs, a relative of the Maharajah, and one of her servants, to whom he had offered personal violence with his own hands. In one of these cases, Mr. Rungacharloo was fined Rs. 100, and in the other, Rs. 200. On appeal, however, he pleaded that he was acting in his "political" capacity, and that the precincts of the palace were exempt from the jurisdiction of the courts. The Chief Commissioner upheld the plea, and the judgments were quashed. On the other hand, it must, in justice to Mr. Rungacharloo, be stated that in cases of this description, he has not always been the assailant. He was, very soon after being thus relieved by special dispensation from the legal consequences of his own stern system of discipline, himself severely slippered within the walls of the Palace by some of the Ranee's retainers, and when the culprits were brought by him before the magistrate, they were not allowed to plead that they lived in a royal Alsatia, but were treated as ordinary offenders against the law. Unfortunately, no punishment can wipe out a slippering. In India, the fact of having been slippered, even unjustly, derogates from a man's dignity and renders him incurably ridiculous. And in this case, public sympathy in Mysore, most unofficially perverse and prejudiced, was on the side of the delinquents.

These were some of the incidents, it may be assumed, which led your predecessors, Mr. Saunders and Sir Richard Meade, to blame Colonel Malleson, the Guardian, for having "left too much power in the hands of" Mr. Rungacharloo, "an official of undoubted ability and integrity, but greatly disliked by the Ranees and their dependants".*

The brief survey we have taken of some of his judicial experiences, well deserving a more detailed scrutiny, but probably unmentioned in your official report on his merits, would hardly impress anyone quite unversed in the ways of Anglo-Indian administration with a strong conviction as to Mr. Rungacharloo's personal dignity, or as to the likelihood of his being influential and popular in the Mysore territories. You, however, must have cared for none of these things, or must have acquired some knowledge or some belief as to Mr. Rungacharloo's acceptability and popularity unknown to your predecessors, for you presented him to the Viceroy of India in Council, in 1879, as "the fittest person in the Province for the appointment" of Minister, and as "being preferred by the Maharajah to any others who might be nominated".† "Mr. Gordon," you say "has consulted the Maharajah on the point." "The names of all officers employed in Mysore, who are in any way eligible for the place, have been deliberately laid before the Maharajah, and he has expressed his undoubted preference for Mr. Rungacharloo."‡

---

* Despatch in the Secret Department from the Viceroy, Lord Lytton, in Council, to the Secretary of State for India, dated "Simla, 3rd May 1877", paragraph 8.

† *Mysore Papers*, No. 1 of 1881, pp. 182 and 187.   ‡ *Ib.*, p. 187.

And yet you had at this time recommended to the Government of India, as "absolutely necessary", not only that the nomination to the office of Minister should be reserved for the Government " by means of the power of approval or veto",* but also that it was " most desirable to make this intention known in unequivocal terms, rather than to leave it as a matter of inference, as has not unfrequently been the practice elsewhere".† I should be surprised, therefore, to hear that you had not made "this intention known" in good time to the young Maharajah, " in unequivocal terms".

Two years before the Maharajah's installation, you had also obtained permission from the Government of India to place Mr. Rungacharloo in the position of your Secretary " to be trained for the office of Dewan", " in close relation with yourself".‡ I should be very much surprised to hear that this fact was not made known in good time to the young Maharajah, by yourself or by the Dewan designate, " in terms quite unequivocal", even if indirectly conveyed.

Under the circumstances, very sufficiently revealed in the Blue Book, I cannot admit the possibility of the Maharajah, eighteen years old, secluded from converse or contact with any of the notables of his country, with Mr. Rungacharloo as *Maire du Palais* during the whole of the minority, having ever been allowed to feel that he had a free choice in the matter. I cannot believe that there can have been any great alacrity on the part of Mr. Rungacharloo, or the people appointed by him and in his interest near His Highness's person, to reassure the Maharajah as to his right to express a real preference for any particular person as his first Dewan, or an objection to any particular person—to persuade him, in short, that he had a perfect right to celebrate the day of his majority, or to anticipate his emancipation, by flying in the face of the Chief Commissioner and the Viceroy, and rejecting their nominee for the

---

* *Mysore Papers*, No. 1 of 1881, p. 187.
† *Ibid.*, p. 94.   ‡ *Ibid.*, p. 97.

office of Dewan after that nominee had been two years "in training" for the office.

I may seem to have been once more wandering a little from my proper task, which is that of defending myself from your attacks on the Memorandum in the *Statesman*, signed "E. B.", relating to the Mysore Jewels. Mr. Rungacharloo's eligibility for the office of Minister is not entirely irrelevant, but I will return to the main subject.

You have accused me of making "strange misstatements", without pointing out anything of the sort. You have accused me of "garbling documents", without offering a single instance of anything that can have appeared to you in that light. You have, I am aware, made free use of such terms as "a mare's nest", "a weak and easily exposed invention". The *Pioneer*, well known to be officially inspired, called my Memorandum an "unadulterated fiction", and you gave your approval to that somewhat unhappy compound. You accuse me of "weaving a malicious story of spoliation and loss of the Mysore State Jewels". I again defy you to point out anything like malice, either in the moral or the legal sense, in anything I have written. No story of spoliation or loss originated with me. In the Memorandum signed "E. B.", official records are quoted proving an unexplained and unreported loss of value in the jewels between the completion of the catalogue by Colonel Elliot in 1868 and the rearrangement by yourself and Mr. Rungacharloo in 1872. Your own official Note of the 5th September 1877 is quoted, in which you state that in July 1872 you found "a great number of such inaccuracies". The most remarkable among "the great number" of unreported "inaccuracies", was that of a jewel, No. 32, which, although catalogued by Major Elliot in 1868 as worth Rs. 6,000 (say £600), "appeared small" in 1872, and was found only to be worth about Rs. 600 (say £60). Your Committee of November 1880 report a similar discrepancy in the value of another jewel, No. 171, from the same collection, allotted to the same widow Chundra Vilasa, who died in June

1871, about a year before the rearrangement which you commenced in July 1872. Thus there is ample evidence that before that rearrangement the jewels had been feloniously reduced in value. To what extent they have been reduced cannot be told without a revaluation. I wrote my original Memorandum signed "E. B.", knowing nothing of the second remarkable "inaccuracy", No. 171. But when you and Mr. Rungacharloo are now compelled to acknowledge, in contradiction to your previous denials, that the valuable jewel so numbered was abstracted and replaced by an inferior article, I consider myself justified in still explaining, by the same process of "abstraction and substitution", the reduction of Jewel No. 32 of the same Chundra Vilasa collection from its estimated value of Rs. 6,000 (£600) to the actual value of Rs. 600 (£60). That was the opinion expressed in the Memorandum signed "E. B.", and it is verified by your Committee of November 1880. The explanation you at first preferred of "a merely clerical error" is now totally inadmissible.

What I did in the Memorandum signed "E. B." was not, as you misrepresent it, "to make specific statements as to losses", not to make charges against anyone, but to affirm the existence of a scandal and to call for an investigation.

I considered it my duty, in the last paragraph of my Memorandum, after pointing out what seemed to me to be grave reasons for an independent inquiry, to urge that "if the very same functionaries who had been singled out by circumstances for sole responsibility, were to be left unprotected by any inquiry or supervision, to hand over to the young Maharajah, by their own method and process, property valued in 1868 at more than £350,000, and virtually to grant themselves an acquittance, the seed would be sown for future crops in mischievous rotation of incurable scandals and unanswerable claims". The very course which I humbly ventured to deprecate has been pursued. No independent inquiry has been made; no precautions have been taken.

The course which I suggested would have been—as I fully expect some of your own friends will tell you by the time they have read this Letter—the best one for your own protection. You took my intervention, however, in bad part, and have reduced me to the necessity of protecting myself. You felt secure, and, as it appears, on good grounds, of being officially supported; and of no weight being given to an unauthorised and irregular warning. You have been allowed to hand over to the young Maharajah, without valuation, property valued in 1868 at more than £350,000. You as Resident, late Chief Commissioner, and Mr. Rungacharloo as Minister, late Controller of the Household, have exchanged mutual acquittances. The Government of India confirms, approves, and is quite satisfied. Kanchi Rungachari is sent, for a year, to gaol. The Residency Sheristadar, wrongly suspected of giving me information, is dismissed by you, without a pension, after twenty-three years' service. You are made a Knight of the Star of India. If Mr. Rungacharloo were only exalted to the same dignity, I suppose my confusion ought to be complete. But I am not confused, or confuted. I still maintain that for your sake an independent inquiry, and a revaluation of the Mysore State Jewels, were very desirable.

In the Memorandum signed "E. B.", I pointed out that any examination of the jewels would be delusive and inconclusive, and would fail to clear away the scandalous rumours that had prevailed for seven years, unless it were, as recommended by Captain F. A. Wilson in 1877, conducted by "a special agency" of unquestionable independence. I urged also that, as the injurious report was, as ineffectually hinted by Captain F. A. Wilson in 1877, that "jewels" had not always been "restored to the jewel-room in the same state in which they were taken out"*—that they had been, in short, "sweated"—the great object of inquiry must be a revaluation of the jewels, to be compared with the careful estimate made by Major Elliot and Mr. Rungacharloo, with a jury of experts, in 1868.

* *Mysore Papers*, No. 1 of 1881, p. 150.

This, perhaps, is the most appropriate place to mention that the story current in Mysore, as told to me, is that if the Jewels were now to be revalued, it would be found that at least one-sixth, if not one-fifth, of their value, had evaporated,—the Jewel-room property being, it is said, diminished in about the same proportion as the Wardrobe property was, confessedly, diminished in Mr. Rungacharloo's charge. You may call the story a legend,—you may call it a myth,—but it is the refusal of inquiry that converts these myths or legends into articles of popular faith.

Your opinion as to a special and independent inquiry, and as to a revaluation, differed entirely from mine. You considered, and your course has been approved by the authorities at Calcutta, that no valuation was required, and that it would be enough to call together a Committee composed of those among your subordinates who had been connected with Palace affairs, including Mr. C. Rungacharloo, and to preside over it yourself. For thus constituting the Committee you gave the curious reason that "as no examination of the jewellery had been made since that conducted by Mr. Gordon in 1872, and as such specific statements had been made of losses that had occurred since the original examination of 1868, it was thought to be very desirable that, at the present examination, all the officers in India who had at any time since the Maharajar's death had charge of the jewellery should be present".* Of course they ought to have been present as witnesses, but not as judges.

It is clear that you perfectly understood what you were doing in thus packing the Committee, although its impropriety did not strike you, because you conclude your despatch of the 18th of December 1880, by declaring your confidence that "it will be seen how utterly unfounded are the statements which have been so industriously circulated, and how thoroughly satisfied all the responsible officers concerned are as to the complete identity and accuracy of the jewels", and by

* *Mysore Papers*, No. 1 of 1881, p. 166.

expressing your "trust that the results of the examination now reported will satisfy His Excellency the Viceroy in Council that there is not any ground whatever for ascribing to the responsible officers in Mysore, in the past or present, any neglect in the preservation of the Mysore State jewels".*

Doubts having been set forth "as to the complete identity and accuracy of the jewels", "specific statements having been made as to losses", "neglect" having been ascribed to "the responsible officers", you think it quite enough that "the responsible officers" concerned should combine to declare themselves "thoroughly satisfied" with their own conduct.

Even this does not fully convey the utter nullity of this pretended inquiry by your subordinates. For the real question, after all, was not *their* conduct, but *yours*. Not one of the subordinate officials, whom you and Mr. Rungacharloo paraded at Mysore in November 1880, had ever been "in charge of the jewellery". Not one of them had taken any part in the unsanctioned and unreported rearrangement of 1872. You and Mr. Rungacharloo, and you two only, are "the responsible officers".

Mr. Krishna Murti says:—"I never had charge of the jewellery at any time."† He acted as Controller of the Household, under the Tutor, Captain (now Major) F. A. Wilson, while Mr. Rungacharloo was absent on leave—at a very critical time, as we shall see—in 1877.

Mr. Sheshadri Iyer acted as Controller, under Colonel Hay, in 1878 and 1879, and "had no exclusive charge of the Palace jewellery".‡

Mr. Ananda Rao says:—"I have not at any time had immediate charge of the Palace jewellery." He was only Assistant-Commissioner superintending the Household under Colonel Hay, from May 1879.§

Colonel Hay only answers for his "general charge of the Palace duties" since April 1879.‖

---

* *Mysore Papers*, No. 1 of 1881, p. 167.   † *Ibid.*, p. 171.
‡ *Ibid.*, p. 177.   § *Ibid.*, p. 178.   ‖ *Ibid.*, p. 169.

To these disclaimers of responsibility there is one apparent exception. Major F. A. Wilson, who, "although invited, was unable to attend" at Mysore, writes from Hyderabad:—"As Tutor to His Highness the Maharaja, I was in charge of the Guardian's office from July 1876 till relieved by Mr. Gordon early in 1878, and, in that capacity, had charge of the Palace jewellery, holding in my possession the key of an iron safe (under a sentry), in which were deposited the keys of the jewel-room and of the cases containing the jewellery."* He had, in short, from July 1876, to February 1878, been in charge of the master-key. That is all he means.

It does not appear, and I certainly do not assert, that even you were ever in "exclusive" or "immediate" charge of the jewellery.

Out of the seven persons, yourself included, whose signatures or depositions are attached to the report of November 1880, only *one* was "at any time since the Maharajah's death", in "immediate" and "exclusive" charge of the Palace jewellery. This was Mr. Rungacharloo. He was, from July 1869 to May 1879, "vested with authority in the Palace", over all "the various departments."† He alone kept the key of the wardrobe. He had charge of the "jewellery in daily use of the several departments", as Colonel Malleson states in his letter to the Chief Commissioner of the 22nd of December 1874.‡ In addition to this jewellery in daily use, often amounting to "a lakh of rupees, or more, in value", which had to "remain out for days and months", there was "jewellery of the value of some lakhs of rupees", left out for the use of "the Dowager Maharanis, and other ladies", from the time of Colonel Elliot's settlement until the decease of those ladies. Thus, during several years, jewels, "of the value of some lakhs of rupees", including the "especially large" collection of the Ranee Chundra Vilasa, were subject to the absolute control of Mr. Rungacharloo. He does, indeed, assert, in his deposition, that "in every instance of the death

---

* *Mysore Papers*, No. 1 of 1881, p. 170.
† *Papers, Mysore Government*, 385 of 1878, p. 130.
‡ Appendix A.

of these Maharanis and ladies, the jewellery was completely accounted for.* But that assertion, as will be seen, is falsified by this very Report of November 1880, and by other official records that will be cited; and the extent or limits of that falsification can only be defined by a revaluation of the jewels.

Mr. Rungacharloo, moreover, and he alone, had, as we shall see, the master-key in his possession, for days and weeks together, without the check or supervision of any English officer.

Let us now recapitulate what you did in October 1880. You "invited" six officials to form a Committee of Inquiry into the condition of the Mysore jewels, on the strange ground that they had all been in charge of the jewels. You called on these officers to assume a judicial position, when they were obviously disqualified as judges. You called on them to come forward as witnesses to matters of which they were, with one exception, necessarily ignorant. Not one of them, with the exception of Mr. Rungacharloo, had been even in partial or temporary charge of the jewels before July 1876. But all the "specific statements" as to "losses" with which you had to deal, referred to misfortunes or malpractices before the completion of your unsanctioned rearrangement of the jewels in July 1872. It was then, according to your official note of September 5th, 1877, that you discovered a jewel (No. 32 of the Chundra Vilasa collection) valued in 1868 at Rs. 6,000 (£600) to be only worth a tenth of that sum, about Rs. 600 (£60), and found, likewise, "a great number of such inaccuracies". Another article from the same Chundra Vilasa collection (No. 171), a diamond bracelet, valued at Rs. 5,000 (£500), was found by the Committee of 1880 to be only worth about Rs. 2,000 (£200). The report adds :—"It is believed in the Palace that the relations of the lady substituted an inferior jewel whilst it was in her possession."†

The statement as to belief "in the Palace" is one that is very easily made, but being made by the very

* *Mysore Papers*, No. 1 of 1881, p. 174. † *Ibid.*, p. 168.

person who must be more or less responsible and blameworthy, at least for any irregularities or negligence that may have facilitated malpractices, this vague reference to invisible and anonymous culprits can hardly be considered conclusive by any one. It must be taken for what it is worth, as an excuse put forward by Mr. Rungacharloo, who was for ten years " vested with authority over all the departments" of the Palace. It is manifestly worth nothing, and less than nothing, as a proof of what you claim to have established, " that the arrangements for the preservation of the Palace jewellery have been, since the original registration in 1868, carefully and duly observed".* But it is worth a great deal as a proof, extracted from your packed Committee, that between 1868 and 1872 the process of "abstraction and substitution" was actually employed as a means of depredation on the Maharajah's jewels. "Abstraction and substitution" are the words I used in paragraph 14 of the Memorandum, signed "E. B".† You protested against them, and charged me with " strange misstatements" as to a supposed loss of jewels.‡ In the last paragraph but one of your Memorandum, dated the 29th of July 1880, offered to the Government of India as a full and sufficient answer to my Memorandum on the Mysore jewels, you " have no hesitation in assuring the Government that, notwithstanding the inconvenience occasioned by the large quantities of jewellery frequently required for the use of the Maharaja and the Maharani, *there is no reason whatever to believe that any loss or malpractices have taken place*".§

In July you declare " any loss or malpractice" to be incredible. In November 1880, you had to report a " loss" of £300 in value on one item, by the very " malpractice" of "abstraction and substitution" suggested in my Memorandum, and which four months before you had " no hesitation" in declaring incredible.

You and your subordinates had also to admit in that same report of November 1880 that this instance of

---

* *Mysore Papers*, No. 1 of 1881, p. 168.
† *Ibid.*, p. 144.   ‡ *Ibid.*, p. 146.   § *Ibid.*, p. 149.

abstraction and substitution was discovered "when that lady", the Ranee Chundra Vilasa, "died, in 1871". It must, therefore, have formed one of the "great number of inaccuracies" of which you took note in your rearrangement and "fresh lists" of July 1872, and which you reserved *in petto*, until one of them was accidentally revealed in 1877.

We learn, also, from your Committee of November 1880, that out of a parcel of thirty-eight diamonds, No. 566, valued in the original catalogue at Rs. 1,500, twenty-four were wanting. "This deficiency", a deficiency in value, on one item, of about £100, "had been noticed in the examination of 1872."* It may have been noticed, but it was not reported, either to the Chief Commissioner, or to Colonel Malleson. There is no suggestion of a clerical error, but you say:—"It will probably be found on inquiry that they have been used in repairs of other jewels."† This simply means that this deficiency of £100 in value is not accounted for, that it is not traced, and that no one is held responsible for it.

There is another little parcel that the Committee of November 1880, returns as "not found":—"No. 544. Six loose addikes (links) belonging to a pounchi (bracelet), value Rs. 600. It is a question whether our not finding No. 544 is due to a mistake in the original list of 1868, or to its being mixed up with other jewels, as in 1868 it was recorded as consisting of loose pieces of a broken jewel."‡

This, likewise, being translated into the vulgar tongue, means that another item, No. 544, valued at £60, is not accounted for, is not traced, and that no one is held responsible for it.

Mr. Krishna Murti, also, informs us, by the way, of another lost jewel, no mention of which appears anywhere else, and the value of which is not stated. "One jewel", he says, "was accounted for as having been stolen in the Palace Treasure burglary;"§ one of the

---

* *Mysore Papers*, No. 1 of 1881, p. 168.
† *Ibid.*, p. 168.   ‡ *Ibid.*, p. 168.   § *Ibid.*, p. 173.

incidents called by that name which recur so frequently during Mr. Rungacharloo's Controllership, without apparently exciting more than a languid curiosity in any official bosom.

These "facts now reported", after an eight days' hasty examination, and, as Mr. Krishna Murti innocently betrays to us, without any "valuation", by no means "establish conclusively" to my mind, that there is any weight in your assurance as "Chief Commissioner", "that this valuable property has been throughout preserved with the strictest fidelity and care".*

On the contrary, no one can now deny that the annals of the Controller's Department during the last nine years testify to the accuracy of the "specific statements" regarding "losses" of some of "the very valuable property kept in the Palace", and to some remarkable deficiencies in its value, as estimated and recorded in 1868.

The Wardrobe was entirely and exclusively in Mr. Rungacharloo's charge, as we learn from Colonel Malleson's letter to the Chief Commissioner, of the 22nd of December 1874.† The Wardrobe was estimated by Colonel Elliot and Mr. Rungacharloo in 1868 to be worth about £25,000.‡ Before the end of 1874, as we are told by Sir Richard Meade, the Chief Commissioner, in his Order dated the 30th of November in that year, Mr. Rungacharloo had managed to lose about a sixth part of this "very valuable property"—clothes to the value of at least £4,000 having disappeared in a series of what were called "burglaries". These incidents were very lightly treated by Sir Richard Meade, who did not even know how many had occurred, though he seems to have known that the first of them had never been reported.§ In his Order of the 30th of November 1847, the loss of Rs. 36,000 (£3,500) in one of these "burglaries", does not seem to strike him as a matter

---

* *Mysore Papers*, No. 1 of 1881, p. 167.
† Appendix A.
‡ *Mysore Government*, 385 of 1878, p. 91.
§ I have heard that there were no less than five of these "burglaries."

of great moment, though he censures Mr. Rungacharloo for "supineness" and "inadequate action" on the loss being discovered.

In this respect your tone and touch throughout, both as Guardian and as Chief Commissioner, are quite in harmony with Sir Richard Meade's instrument. Having discovered in 1872 "a great number" of such discrepancies between the actual value of jewels and the estimate formed by a jury of experts in 1868, as reduced them to a fraction of their recorded value, you did not consider this discovery of sufficient importance to be either made known "at the time", or at any time, to your official superior, the Chief Commissioner, or communicated, on his return, to Colonel Malleson, the Guardian, for whom you were acting, or to anyone else who was in a position to institute a serious inquiry.

Again, having in July 1880, denied that "any loss or malpractices had taken place,"* you admit both loss and malpractice in November 1880,† but pronounce the "differences" arising therefrom to be "slight" and immaterial."‡ Deficiences of £540, £300, £100, and £60 in the value of single items in the list of jewellery, (No. 32, 171, 566, and 544)§ may be considered by you to be "slight" and "immaterial"; they would hardly seem so in the eye of an ordinary man of business. They would certainly not be so accounted either in the Viceroy's Tosha-khana, or in the jewel-room of a reigning Rajah; but in the Palace of Mysore the Viceroy had no concern, and the Rajah had no control.

Mr. C. Rungacharloo is in complete accordance with you as to the "slight" and "immaterial" nature of the deficiencies in value.

"The result of the examination", he says, "was that all the jewels have been fully accounted for; the four or five items of differences found in articles of trifling value, some in excess and others by way of deficiency, were such as must be expected from the confused manner in which numerous petty articles have been

---

* *Ante*, p. 21.
‡ *Mysore Papers*, No. 1 of 1881, p. 167.
† *Ante*, pp. 21, 22.
§ *Ante*, pp. 21, 22.

mixed up with the larger jewels in the original registration."*

He thus professes to consider such articles as a seven-string necklace (No. 32) valued at £600, and a diamond bracelet valued at £500, to be "of trifling value", and "the four or five items of difference"—such as £540 on No. 32, £300 on No. 171, £100 on No. 566, and £60 on No. 544—to be "such as must be expected". The whole of this answer will be seen to be irreconcilable with the facts. The jewels in which deficiencies appear are not "of trifling value", and were not in any instance "mixed up" with "petty articles."

Nor is Mr. Rungacharloo's plea of petty articles "in excess", to counterbalance deficiencies, admissible. No excess worth speaking of appears; nor would any such excess do away with the acknowledged abstraction and substitution in the instances of No. 32 and No. 171,—instances which might, for all that we can know until Mr. Krishna Murti's "proper valuation" is instituted, be greatly multiplied.

Mr. Sheshadri Iyer, one of Mr. Rungacharloo's lieutenants, brings forward, likewise, this groundless plea of an "excess". He echoes your assurances of July 1880, in the following words:—"I have no hesitation in saying that the whole of the palace jewellery, as per Colonel Elliot's list of 1868, has been fully and satisfactorily accounted for." And he gives as his reason for this conclusion, that although some "articles of small value" may not be forthcoming, "on the other hand, an excess was found, consisting of loose pearls and precious stones and sundry small articles of jewellery, and this would, in my opinion, to a great extent account for the deficiencies above referred to."† It is perfectly clear, for the reasons already given, that it would not account for any one of the serious deficiencies.

The truth is, that in reviewing your proceedings of November 1880, even the discrepancies regarding the value of jewels therein acknowledged, are not as re-

* *Mysore Papers*, No. 1 of 1881, pp. 175, 176.
† *Ibid.* p. 178.

markable as the discrepancies between the acknowledgments of the "Joint Report", and the denials that each separate member of the packed Committee gives in his answers to your eight leading questions.

Mr. C. Rungacharloo says:—" I have no reason to suspect any irregularities of any kind. Everything has been so completely and accurately accounted for."*

Mr. T. Ananda Rao says:—"I have found no sufficient reason to suspect that a less valuable jewel has been fraudulently substituted for a more valuable one, or that any jewel has been altered for the purpose of diminishing its value."†

Mr. K. Sheshadri Iyer says:—" I have no reason whatever to suspect any fraudulent substitution or alteration of any jewel."‡

Colonel A. C. Hay says:—"Opinions may differ as to the absolute correctness of the valuation of the jewels, but there is no reason to suspect that any fraudulent substitutions or alterations have been made."§

And this although they had just signed, or were about to sign, the Report declaring a flagrant instance of fraudulent substitution and alteration, discovered by you and Mr. Rungacharloo in 1872, and unrevealed until 1880.

You had "no hesitation", in July 1880, in pronouncing the notion of "any loss or malpractices" to be quite incredible, and in expressing your "confident belief" in the "scrupulous care and fidelity" with which the jewels had been preserved.|| Your "want of hesitation" is reproduced, and your "confident belief" is repeated, for the most part, as we have just seen, in the answers given separately by the members of the Committee, who collectively, in their "Joint Report", admit the occurrence of both "loss and malpractice". But even amidst this inconsistent unanimity there are some perceptible reservations. Major F. A. Wilson, for example, in his reply to Question 2, seems to be more anxious than the other deponents to give no opinion as

---

* *Mysore Papers*, No. 1 of 1881, p. 176. † *Ibid.*, p. 179.
‡ *Ibid.*, p. 177.   § *Ibid.*, p. 170. || *Ibid.*, p. 149.

to occurrences beyond the limits of the time when he was acting as Tutor to the Maharajah. He says:—" I cannot remember ever to have heard or in any way become aware of any irregularity or impropriety in connexion with the palace jewellery during the period of my charge."*

Having made answer so far, he does not seem to have considered himself called upon to say anything with reference to the second part of Question 2, requesting him to state " in detail", whether he took any "action", in consequence of "information" received as to irregularities. I shall have immediately to show that Major Wilson *did* take very effective *"action"* for the better security of the jewels. He may have done so without any information, and without any rumours as to previous irregularities; but this is by no means clear, and is in itself highly improbable. It would seem rather that at the critical moment of 1877, Major F. A. Wilson, or some one at his elbow, was on the verge of avowing suspicion. The following sentence from paragraph 6 of the Tutor's letter of 21st August 1877, looks very much as if he suspected that there had been some previous malpractices or negligence in the department:—" Care is, however, *at present*, taken to see that jewels taken out are restored to the jewel-room in the same state in which they were taken out."† This hint covers nearly the whole ground of the scandals that have long been prevalent in Mysore, as to the abstraction and substitution of jewels,—well founded scandals as we now know from the reluctant acknowledgments that my pressure has forced from you and your select Committee of 1880.

Mr. Krishna Murti, and Mr. Ananda Rao, whose position and connections, as I understand, secure them from being entirely dependent on the goodwill of Mr. Rungacharloo, do not seem to me to join in the chorus of general content with the same vigour and fervour as Mr. Sheshadri Iyer. They guard themselves with

* *Mysore Papers*, No. 1 of 1881, p. 170.
† *Ibid.*, No. 1, p. 150.

qualifications, and they let out little facts of considerable significance, that we do not find anywhere else. Between them, they open our eyes to the path and the process by which the "malpractices" of "abstraction and substitution", denied in your own despatches, but admitted in the "Joint Report", where their subdued voices are heard,—may have been carried on, and to the possibility that these "malpractices" may have been much more extensive than you are inclined to believe.

"The main stock of jewellery", says Mr. Ananda Rao, "is kept in a room on the first floor of the Palace, not far from the Maharajah's sleeping apartments, and quite accessible from the zenana apartments of the palace."* "Quite accessible from the zenana,"—let us take note of that. The room is described by Mr. Krishna Murti as being "in the middle of the Palace buildings, surrounded on all sides by several sets of rooms and walls. There are no approaches to it from outside, except through the usual passage. So, therefore, the best room available for the purpose has been utilized." (That opinion as to its being "the best room for the purpose," is rather awkwardly placed, considering what follows.) "This room", he continues, " had, when it was first opened during my Controllership, *three doors, two of which in the side walls were, I learnt, only chained from inside, while the third main door was locked and sealed from outside. Captain Wilson and I took the additional precaution of putting on locks to the two side doors. Since then I see the doors have been, as was thought desirable by us, shut up and walls raised.*"†

And here is Major Wilson's testimony as to the same point :—" *Two side doors of the jewel room, secured on the inside but not locked, of which I had previously been unaware, came to my notice on one of these occasions. These doors were, under my directions, provided with locks,* as I considered their condition out of harmony with the otherwise generally rigid arrangements

---

* *Mysore Papers*, No. 1 of 1881, p. 178.   † *Ibid.*, p. 172.

for the safe custody of the jewels, which were in my opinion efficient and satisfactory."*

This very peculiar arrangement of doors was, therefore, not considered by Major Wilson and Mr. Krishna Murti to be either "efficient" or "satisfactory" "for the safe custody of the jewels", and they had it altered. Yet Mr. Rungacharloo had been satisfied with it for eight years, and you—if it was ever brought to your notice—could not have considered it objectionable. But I think the Tutor and the Acting Controller were more discreet than you and Mr. Rungacharloo. The caution evinced by Mr. Krishna Murti, and the "action taken" by Major F. A. Wilson, when they found out the double back-entry, "quite accessible from the zenana", into the jewel-room, in addition to the front or formal entry, seem to me to have been most judicious. Unfortunately, they came a little too late. Your own official Note of the 5th of September 1877, and the Report of your Committee of November 1880, prove that it was a case of shutting the stable-door when the steed was stolen. The very imperfect revelations called forth by my Memorandum in the *Statesman*—very imperfect in the absence of Mr. Krishna Murti's "proper valuation"—show that the felonious alteration of No. 32 and No. 171, causing a loss of £840 in value in two items, and the disappearance of twenty-four diamonds worth £100, from No. 566, besides other similar "slight and immaterial differences", all occurred before you inaugurated the "great improvement", as you call it, of new bureaus and Chubb's locks in 1872. Mr. Krishna Murti and Major F. A. Wilson introduced a still greater improvement when they locked the two superfluous doors; but it was too late. The Chubb's locks, the master-key and the seals, before and after 1872, are exposed as a mere sham safeguard, when we know that by the dexterous detachment of a chain from a hook, during an official visit, the jewel-room could at any time have been left open to clandestine and predatory incursions. Mr. Ananda Rao and Mr.

* *Mysore Papers*, No. 1 of 1881, p. 171.

Krishna Murti, between them, explain how the jewel-room was "quite accessible", and could be got at through "the Zenana", where we know there was at least one inmate, Murree Mullapa, familiar with the ways of the place, and well qualified for participating in the work of "abstraction and substitution". Nothing but the "proper valuation", for which Mr. Krishna Murti calls, can reveal how far that work had proceeded in 1872, beyond such instances as No. 32 and No. 171, which are no longer to be denied or disputed, but which you now call "slight and immaterial".

In the course of the proceedings of your Committee of November 1880, you do not offer any explanation, or even a remark, regarding these two doors, masked inside and unfastened outside until 1877. You probably considered this circumstance, like the deficiency of £1,000 in four items of jewellery, to be "slight and immaterial". And perhaps when the date of Major Wilson's and Mr. Krishna Murti's precautions is considered, you would be, in a certain sense, right.

Mr. Rungacharloo, likewise, is silent as to the doors. He thinks it quite enough to "appeal in regard to the success of" his "arrangements" "to the high and strict *morale*" maintained by him in the Palace.* We have Mr. Rungacharloo's word for this "high and strict *morale*", and for "the success of his arrangements", which are not, however, made brilliantly manifest by the fact that when Mr. Rungacharloo had been for five years in direct and exclusive charge of the Palace Wardrobe, one-sixth of that property, to the value of at least £4,000, was lost.

Mr. Rungacharloo, having attributed "the success of his arrangements" to the "*morale*" prevailing in the Palace under his fostering care, remembers that there was one person in the Palace, very frequently mentioned in the *Statesman*, very closely associated with himself, whose "*morale*", instead of being "high and strict", was notoriously low and loose. This was Murree

* *Mysore Papers*, C 3,026 of 1881, p. 175.

Mullapa. Mr. Rungacharloo makes a show of taking the bull by the horns. Alluding to this man, he says:—"I must, however, specially refer to one of the leading subordinate officials who was connected with the jewellery department of the Palace till his death some six years ago."

It is remarkable that, at the outset, Mr. Rungacharloo should misplace the date of this person's death. Murree Mullapa did not die about *six*, but about *nine* years before November 1880. Mr. Rungacharloo, nevertheless, had many reasons to recollect this death, and the circumstances connected with it. Murree Mullapa died in December 1871, six months after the widowed Ranee Chundra Vilasa, in whose "especially large" collection of jewels we have found some striking deficiencies. About six months after Murree Mullapa's death you commenced, in July 1872, that rearrangement of the jewels during which some of those deficiencies were observed, but not reported.

"This man, named Murree Mullapa," continues Mr. Rungacharloo, "was an influential and important official under the late Maharajah, and was chiefly in charge of the jewellery department under him. His reputation was not of the best kind, as indeed was the case with several of the higher officials in the Palace, who were exposed to the corrupting influences and intrigues carried on in the former *régime*, a misfortune which did not so much affect the smaller officials. He was retained by Colonel Elliot, as by long experience he was useful, and the Maharanis would have objected to the removal of so old a servant."

The truth I believe to be that Colonel Elliot, who was well aware of the man's infamous character, did not appoint him, and would not have retained him, if he could have exercised any choice in the matter. The Maharanis were never consulted. The only person who found Murree Mullapa's "experience useful", and wanted him, was Mr. Rungacharloo. Colonel Elliot, in fact, was not strong enough, any more than was Colonel Gregory Haines, the Guardian chosen by the old Maharajah and the Secretary of State, to get the man removed.*

I return to Mr. Rungacharloo's apology for Murree Mullapa. "I can only say that whatever he had been, he was guilty of no misconduct in connection with the jewellery department during the time I was employed in the Palace."

Mr. Rungacharloo having already declared that there was "no reason to suspect any irregularities of any kind",† can, of course, express no suspicion of any particular person.

"Indeed," continues Mr. Rungacharloo, "the arrangement was such, and there were so many people jointly responsible, that any irregularity on the part of any one individual was not feasible."

There we are quite in accord. I certainly do not believe that "any individual" alone or single-handed, carried out the work of "abstraction and substitution".

But, according to Mr. Rungacharloo, this pander and poisoner, who was regarded with such dread and horror that, in the words of Colonel Haines, the people "spoke of him with bated breath" made a fine end, and went off in the odour of sanctity.

"I may add that even this individual was so influenced by the altered tone and ideas that he bequeathed almost the whole of his property for the education and improvement of his castemen."‡

Mr. Rungacharloo hardly does himself justice by omitting all mention of his own share in these pious dispositions, and of the subsequent vexations imposed upon himself. The records of the several suits brought against him in the Civil Courts of Mysore by the widow of Murree Mullapa, not settled before the end of 1879, prove that the strange intimacy with the horrible parasite from whose contaminating presence Colonel Haines tried in vain to protect the Maharajah, terminated by Mr. Rungacharloo dictating a death-bed codicil to Murree Mullapa's will, and undertaking its

---

* *Ante*, p. 6. † *Ante*, p. 26.
‡ *Mysore Papers*, C 3,026 of 1881, p. 175.

execution, whereby the widow was prevented from adopting a son, and reduced to a mere maintenance out of the estate, while Mr. Rungacharloo became custodian of the property, including a large amount in jewels.

Thus we see that, besides the unexplained loss of one sixth of the Wardrobe, to the value of £4,000, there are two singular, not to say sinister, facts in the history of Mr. Rungacharloo's nine years' Controllership, on which no light is thrown—the dark doors, "quite accessible from the zenana", and his close and intimate alliance with a man of such hideous infamy as Murree Mullapa. As to those two facts, both he and you are quite silent.

And there is a third fact, that of his having held possession of the master-key for days and weeks together, which he denies. In that denial you support him. Mr. Rungacharloo denies that fact in the following sentence of his deposition:—"The jewels were deposited in wooden almirahs in a room in the centre of the Palace, the keys of which were and have ever since been in charge of the Guardian or other European officer in charge of the Palace."* You very decidedly deny that fact in paragraph 5 of your Memorandum of the 29th of July 1880, in reply to the Memorandum on the Mysore Jewels signed " E. B.":—

" I should add," you say, "that the keys of the jewel-room and jewel cases have always been kept in an iron safe in the Palace under a military guard, and that the key of that safe has always been in the hand of the Guardian, or other high European official resident at Mysore."†

Your statement, as well as that of Mr. Rungacharloo, on whose word, I presume, you relied, is inaccurate. On several occasions when the Guardian, Colonel Malleson, was absent on leave or duty, the master-key was handed over to Mr. Rungacharloo, and not to any European official.

Colonel Malleson, on his first arrival at Mysore in

* *Mysore Papers*, No. 1 of 1881, p. 174.   † *Ibid.*, p. 148.

July 1869, received the master-key from Colonel John Campbell, then Commissioner of the Ashtagram Division, into whose charge it had been committed by Colonel Gregory Haines, on his resigning the office of Guardian. The key never again came into the hands of Colonel John Campbell, though he remained at Mysore, holding the same position of Commissioner, until February 1873. He was succeeded by Colonel Thomas Clerk until July 1874, when Colonel A. C. Hay took up the appointment.

When Colonel Malleson left Mysore, in company with the Ursoos, members of the Maharajah's family, in December 1870, to wait on Lord Mayo at Calcutta, the master-key was transferred to Mr. Rungacharloo, and not to Colonel John Campbell, or any other "high European official".

Colonel Malleson proceeded a second time to Calcutta, with the Ursoos, in December 1873, when the master-key was again given to Mr. Rungacharloo—not to Colonel Thomas Clerk, who was then Commissioner of the Division, or to any other high European official—and the key so remained in Mr. Rungacharloo's possession until the Guardian's return in February 1874.

When Colonel Malleson was relieved of the Guardianship in June 1876, he was directed to give over charge to Mr. Rungacharloo, who once more held possession of the master-key for some weeks.

Major F. A. Wilson will be able to satisfy you as to the person from whom he received the key on his arrival at Mysore in August 1876, to take up his appointment as Tutor; and you will find that person to have been Mr. Rungacharloo, and not Colonel A. C. Hay, or any other "high European official". It is, in short, Major F. A. Wilson, Colonel Malleson, Colonel John Campbell, Colonel Thomas Clerk, and Colonel A. C. Hay that I summon to justify my flat contradiction of the assertions made by you and Mr. Rungacharloo that the master-key was always in the hand of the Guardian or other "high European official". I have before me now a note from Colonel Hay to Colonel

Malleson, dated " 61, Lee Park, Blackheath, Oct. 22nd, 1881", in which he says :—

"While you held the office of Guardian at Mysore it never was the practice for you to make over the master-key of the jewel-room to me, and I cannot recall a single instance of your having done so."

You have accused me of having made "strange misstatements", but have totally failed to support or justify that accusation, even in the most trifling point. I have now convicted you of having, in concurrence with Mr. Rungacharloo, misled the Government of India, by a strange misstatement in a matter of the very greatest importance.

In your Memorandum of July 29th, 1880, you say:—
" What I did in the matter of the re-arrangement of the jewels was not done in secret, as asserted, but was duly made known at the time to the Chief Commissioner, Sir Richard Meade."*

I never asserted that the re-arrangement of 1872 was a secret affair, but that it was a highly irregular affair, begun without any official sanction, and finished without any official report. It may not have been a secret affair, and yet, considering the interesting nature of the work, and the long period over which it extended, it seems to have been " made known at the time", "duly" or unduly, to very few people. It was not known to Colonel John Campbell, the Commissioner of the Division, with whom you were in daily social intercourse, and who had himself been for a short time in charge of the jewel-room keys. It was not known to Colonel (now Major-General) James Puckle, then Secretary to the Chief Commissioner, who must have been aware if there had been any official or demi-official communication. It was not known to several other officers of the Mysore Commission, who, in the ordinary course, must have heard of such proceedings, and who, on the other hand, came to hear those pre-

* *Mysore Papers*, No. 1 of 1881, p. 148.

valent rumours as to misappropriation of the Palace jewels, of which you say you never heard anything, "save in the Memorandum published in the *Statesman*".

In March 1872, Major (now Lieutenant-Colonel) Charles Elliot, C.B., who, assisted by Mr. Rungacharloo, had arranged the jewels in 1868, resigned his office as Commissioner of the Mysore Division, and went home, about three months before the rearrangement of the jewels was commenced in July 1872. You had then been for more than a year officiating as Guardian, Colonel Malleson having gone away on leave in March 1871. You entered on a rearrangement of the jewels without consulting the officer who had received the thanks of the Government in 1868 for "the excellent arrangements" he had made "to prevent any spoliation or loss".

You insist upon it, however, that what you "did in the matter" was "duly made known at the time to Sir Richard Meade". The term "at the time" is vague and indefinite. The word "duly" seems to convey an improper assumption. I can conceive no "*due*" mode of making known the rearrangement of property valued at more than £300,000, except that of correspondence duly dated, in which the sanction, the commencement and the conclusion of such an important work would be duly recorded.

We know to a certainty that there is no contemporaneous order, permission, sanction, report or communication, official or demi-official, relating to the six weeks' manipulation of the jewels in 1872, or to the "great number of inaccuracies" alleged to have been then detected by yourself and Mr. Rungacharloo in that original catalogue for which Mr. Rungacharloo had received the thanks of Government.

In your Order of the 14th of March 1881, dismissing the Residency Sheristadar, you declare, likewise, that "Sir Richard Meade, who had been Chief Commissioner in 1872, was familiar with what had then taken place". Here are your exact words in paragraph 6 of that Order :—

"Mr. Gordon did not make any formal or official reply, but returned the Secretary's letter No. 110 at once, with a few words written at the moment on the back of it, mentioning, for the Chief Commissioner's information (Mr. Saunders having become Chief Commissioner in Sir Richard Meade's place, who had been Chief Commissioner in 1872, and was familiar with what had then taken place), that he had rearranged the jewels, and placed them in new and suitable receptacles in 1872, and that during that rearrangement he had noticed errors such as that under notice, though he could not from memory distinctly recall the particulars of the jewel referred to by Captain Wilson."

Your style is not always as lucid as could be wished, and this passage might be taken to mean that Sir Richard Meade was not only "familiar" with the fact that a rearrangement had taken place in 1872, but was also "familiar" with the fact that you had found "a great number of inaccuracies" in the catalogue. But that cannot have been your meaning, because it is clear Sir Richard Meade can never have heard of these "errors".

Even if you were now to throw some light on the very obscure terms, "familiar", "duly", and "at the time", there would still be need of some further explanation. For it is clear that whatever you may have "made known" to Sir Richard Meade, and whenever, and in whatever style, it may have been made known, everything that you "did in the matter of the rearrangement of the jewels", was not made known "at the time", or at any time, to Sir Richard Meade, or to anybody concerned. On the 29th of July 1880, for example, you tell the Government of India that in July 1872 "fresh additional lists of the jewels, in the order of the rearrangement, were made".* This was not "duly made known" to Sir Richard Meade. No fresh list was furnished to the Chief Commissioner. This was not "duly made known" to Colonel G. B. Malleson on his resuming charge of the

* *Mysore Papers*, No. 1 of 1881, p. 148.

office in 1873. It is perfectly certain that neither of these gentlemen—the head of the Mysore Government and the permanent Guardian—was ever informed either of "the great number of inaccuracies" in the old lists, first divulged in 1877, or of the "fresh lists", first mentioned in 1880. For Sir Richard Meade, in paragraph 7, of his Order No. 135, of 30th November 1874, when the "burglaries" from the Wardrobe had suggested some doubt as to "the security of the very valuable property kept in the Palace", calls for "copies of the lists of the property, prepared in 1868, for record in this office, any changes that have taken place being duly noted in them". According to your explanatory Memorandum of July 1880, the whole had been changed, and new lists had been made in July 1872. But not a hint as to "fresh lists" was given to Sir Richard Meade in reply to his requisition in November 1874. On the contrary, Colonel Malleson—*i.e.*, Mr. Rungacharloo—proclaims "the accuracy of the original lists", even to the absence of "a single error".*

It was on the strength, in fact, of Mr. Rungacharloo's assurances, conveyed in the Guardian's letter of the 22nd of December 1874, as to the perfect security of "the whole of this complicated property", proved by not "a single error" having been found during the rearrangement of 1872, that Sir Richard Meade consented in his letter dated the 11th of January 1875, to mitigate the censure he had passed upon the want of care, vigilance, and activity evinced by Mr. Rungacharloo with regard to the Palace "burglaries".

It is remarkable, to say the least, that throughout the proceedings that have seen the light, or have been instituted, in consequence of the casual disclosures of 1877, and of my Memorandum of 1880, less information is derived, and, strange to say, less appears to be demanded, from Mr. Rungacharloo, than from those who must have had less knowledge, and who clearly have less responsibility.

When we review the Report of your "final" Com-

* Appendix A.

mittee of November 1880, we find that Mr. Rungacharloo, the original and permanent keeper of the jewels, tells us very little, while the temporary custodians, Major Wilson, Mr. Krishna Murti, and Mr. Ananda Rao, tell us a great deal.

During that critical period between July and September 1877, when the facts as to the abstraction and substitution of jewels were within reach of the Chief Commissioner, if he had been of an inquiring turn of mind, Mr. Rungacharloo happened to be out of the way—happened, in fact, to go out of the way—just when he might naturally have been called upon to answer questions as to the discrepancies between the actual value of certain jewels, and their value as ascertained by a jury of experts in 1868. Colonel Elliot and Mr. Rungacharloo had certified to the accuracy of the catalogue, and had been thanked by Government for "their excellent arrangements to prevent spoliation and loss". Moreover, Mr. Rungacharloo, speaking through the voice of Colonel Malleson in the letter dated 22nd of December 1874, had assured the Chief Commissioner that during the rearrangement of the jewels in 1872, "the accuracy of the original lists" was "proved" by not "even a single error" being found "in the whole of this complicated property".*

At this time no discrepancies of value, no instances of "abstraction and substitution" had been discovered, or were officially suspected, outside of the department.

And yet, even at this time, it is to be observed that Mr. Rungacharloo, the real custodian of the Wardrobe and Jewel-room, is allowed quietly to assume, in that same letter of December 22nd, 1874, that "the security of property in the Palace" is a mere question of rules and forms, "of the existing arrangements", "made by Major Elliot and approved of by his successors". He is permitted, without any adverse comment, to go very near divesting himself of all personal responsibility. "I am not aware", he says, in conclusion, "that any improvement could be made in them"—the arrange-

* Appendix A.

ments. "If any further instructions are given on the subject, they will be obeyed."* He has, in short, no duty but that of obeying the rules imposed by his responsible superior. Nevertheless, it may be observed, *en passant*, that Sir Richard Meade's 'instructions' for an annual examination of the Jéwels were not 'obeyed'." But in July 1877, discrepancies of value *had* been discovered, and either Major Wilson or the Chief Commissioner, by making inquiries and insisting on answers from the only person present who had been thanked for the original catalogue, and had ever since been in sole charge of the property, might have been put on the scent of the process by which the jewels had been reduced in value.

The two extra doors, "quite accessible from the zenana", were also detected about the same time, and by the same persons, Mr. Krishna Murti and Major F. A. Wilson, in temporary and partial charge. It seems, therefore, to have been an equally unfortunate and notable concurrence of circumstances, —fortuitous, perhaps, but strange,—that just at the crisis when his explanations were wanted, Mr. Rungacharloo should have gone away on leave. The fact is not easily to be gathered from the published papers, but, as you must be aware, is none the less a fact, that when "the Chief Commissioner's proceedings, No. 42, of the 16th June" 1877,† giving sanction to the list of jewels to be presented to Subramanya Urs on the occasion of his marriage, were issued. Mr. Rungacharloo, Controller of the Household, the working head of the Department, was present at Mysore. But during the inquiry that immediately followed into the puzzling deficiency of about £540 in the value of one of the selected articles, Mr. Rungacharloo took his departure, leaving all inquiries and all explanations alike to be made by inexperienced and irresponsible persons. Captain (now Major) F. A. Wilson, the Tutor, presents the scanty intelligence and halting opinions contained in his letter of the 21st of August 1877, as coming,

* Appendix A. † *Mysore Papers*, No. 1 of 1881, p. 149.

not from Mr. Rungacharloo, whose name is not mentioned in it, but from the Jewel Sheristadar Rama Kristnia, a poor fellow on thirty rupees a month, who in your presence, or before Mr. Rungacharloo, would not have dared to call his soul his own. In July 1877, just when Captain F. A. Wilson was going to let out for the first time those discrepancies in value which are now disclosed as the results of abstraction and substitution, "noticed in the examination of 1872",* Mr. Rungacharloo was off, leaving the burden of defence to be borne by Captain Wilson and Mr. Krishna Murti, who were safe in their ignorance, and by you, the Judicial Commissioner of Mysore, and already for several terms Acting Chief Commissioner, who were not only safe, but strong and unimpeachable by your official position.

When you were asked to elucidate the strange fact that Jewel No. 32, valued in 1868 by a jury of experts at £600, was represented in 1877 by an inferior article worth not more than £60, you had not much of an explanation to offer, but it sufficed. Your answer to the reference from the Chief Commissioner was dated the 5th of September 1877, and ran as follows:—

"I revised, and re-arranged, and placed in new receptacles designed by myself, the Palace jewels in July 1872, or about that time. The work was done in my presence, in that of Mr. Rungacharloo, the Controller, and all the Palace officials concerned. It was a work much required. It occupied us for several hours daily for more than six weeks. I found several such errors as that under notice, but at this distance of time, and considering the very great number of jewels and the great number of such inaccuracies, cannot recall the particulars of the jewels referred to herein—5, 9, 77."†

To express astonishment at Mr. C. B. Saunders, the Chief Commissioner, having been satisfied with this answer, might seem a little hard on that gentleman, considering that the very unsatisfactory answers by

* *Ante*, pp. 20, 22.
† *Mysore Papers*, No. 1 of 1881, p. 144.

yourself, Mr. Rungacharloo, and your packed Committee, have satisfied the Viceroy in Council. But I must point out that in 1877, as at every subsequent period, the essentials for a retrospective and comparative inquiry were much more accessible at Mysore than at Calcutta. For example, I do not feel at all sure that the combined appeal of Colonel Malleson and Mr. Rungacharloo to the Chief Commissioner, dated 22nd of December 1874, was ever transmitted to the Government of India, but there it was at Bangalore,—and by no means pushed away into some dark pigeonhole,—when your very unexplanatory Note of the 5th of September 1877, came in. I am a little astonished that the eulogies on "the original lists" by Colonel Malleson and Mr. Rungacharloo, contradicting your assertion of their inaccuracy, should have escaped notice in 1877, because that very correspondence of December 1874 and January 1875, on the subject of the "burglaries" and the neglected order for an annual examination, had been brought before the Chief Commissioner by the Secretary, Colonel Tredway Clarke, in September 1876.* How came it that Colonel Tredway Clarke did not bring these two irreconcileable documents into conjunction in September 1877? If the Secretary was not capable of such very moderate perspicacity, there ought surely to have been some Assistant Secretary, confidential clerk or keeper of records, to bring to the Chief Commissioner's notice that while you declared "a great number of such inaccuracies" as that which reduced jewel No. 32 to a tenth of its recorded value, to have been found in the lists of 1868, when you and Mr. Rungacharloo rearranged the jewels in 1872, Colonel Malleson and Mr. Rungacharloo, referring to that same rearrangement, had certified to "the accuracy of the original lists", and that there was not "even a single error in the whole of this complicated property".

I am, then, a little surprised that the Chief Com-

† See the deposition of B. Ramaswamy Iyengar, Residency Sheristadar, before you on the 26th of August 1880.

missioner was so easily satisfied with your Note of the 5th of September 1877. I am not, on the other hand, at all surprised to observe that since its more public appearance in the Memorandum signed "E. B.", you are much dissatisfied with it yourself,—so dissatisfied that you have made an example of an innocent victim on account of that publication. Your Note, lightly and indifferently glanced at by Colonel Tredway Clarke and Mr. C. B. Saunders, assumed a very different aspect when brought by me into the light of day, and placed in due relation with other documents. So at least it seems to have struck you, for on every subsequent occasion you have cried it down, sought to modify and minimise its meaning, and even to make it mean the very reverse of its obvious purport. In your Memorandum of the 29th of July 1880, paragraph 2, you term it "no official report", "but a few words on the back of the letter".* In paragraph 4 you say that you "wrote a few remarks from memory upon Captain Wilson's letter".† In paragraph 6 of your Order of the 14th of March 1881, condemning and dismissing the Sheristadar, you say that you "did not make any formal or official reply, but returned the letter at once with a few words written at the moment on the back of it".

My experience of such matters does not show me anything informal, unofficial, or unusual in the mode or language of your Note. Certainly its consisting of a "few words", its being written "at once", "at the moment", and "from memory", did not make it informal or unofficial in the eyes of the Chief Commissioner, Mr. Saunders. If he considered the brevity and promptitude of a reply to be an official merit and the best of formalities, I think he was right.

You say it was written "from memory". Your memory, then, on the 5th of September 1877, told you that during the rearrangement of the jewels begun in July 1872, you and Mr. Rungacharloo had found "a great number of inaccuracies" in the original register

* *Mysore Papers*, No. 1 of 1881, p. 147.
† *Ibid.*, p. 148.

of 1868. Your memory told a different tale when you had to answer my Memorandum signed "E. B." In your Memorandum written with that object, and dated the 29th of July 1880, you say :—

"My belief is that my strong impression at the time I made the re-arrangement (eight years have now elapsed), was that the original register of 1868 was, in all essentials, remarkably accurate; surprisingly so when the circumstances were considered."*

In July 1880, not eight years, but less than three, had elapsed since you wrote "from memory" your statement of September 1877. When you wrote the later statement of July 29th, 1880, your memory told you that "your belief" was that your "strong impression at the time" had been that the original register of 1868 "was, in all essentials, remarkably", even "surprisingly", "accurate". But "at the time", three years before, on the 5th of September 1877, you had written "from memory" that the original register contained "a great number of inaccuracies". Now the probability clearly is that the earlier impression is the more correct, because, though a man might forget in 1880 that he had some years before found inaccuracies in a list, he could not possibly, from any defect of memory, forget himself in 1877 into a belief that he had found "a great number of inaccuracies" in 1872. That would be a freak of fancy, not an effort of memory.

And in fact there was no freak of fancy. Your earlier impression was quite correct. There *were* a great number of inaccuracies in 1872. Such attention as could be given by your select Committee during the eight days' gallop through which you conducted them, without any valuation, brought out some capital specimens of abstraction and substitution, "noticed in the examination of 1872", but not reported, showing a deficiency in value of £1,000 on only four items of jewellery".†

If so much evidence, confirmatory of the scandalous

---

* *Mysore Papers*, No. 1 of 1881, p. 148.
† *Ante*, pp. 20 to 24.

rumours which you proclaimed to be incredible, slipped out in your perfunctory and illusive examination, how much more might not have been extracted by a strict and independent inquiry, and, as Mr. Krishna Murti suggests, by " a proper valuation".

If such an important fact, quite breaking down one buttress in Mr. Rungacharloo's defensive structure, could be drawn out of Colonel A. C. Hay—not, as you will admit, a hostile witness,—by one straightforward question*, how much more light might not have been thrown into dark places, if "the responsible officers in Mysore" had been called upon to meet the "specific statements regarding losses", not by a general chorus in your company, but by separate depositions before an impartial and capable authority!

Although I may be admitted to have shown very conclusively that there were at one time good grounds for a special inquiry; although I may have cleared myself from your charges of "misstatement", "mischievous invention", and the "garbling" of documents, —what object, it may still be asked, can I now have, except one of sheer mischief or malevolence, in stirring up unpleasant matters that have been definitively settled? The Palace Jewels have been transferred from your custody to that of the Maharajah, and the Government of India, in a despatch dated the 26th of May 1881, approve and confirm your proceedings. There is an end of the whole thing. That despatch, with the report and receipt of Basavappajee Urs and five others, on behalf of the Maharajah, has been condescendingly communicated for my information, with reference to two official letters addressed by me to the Indian Government in November and December 1880.† What can I want or expect more?

My last letter in the official correspondence‡ explains why, notwithstanding the approval of Government, I cannot acknowledge your first proceedings in this matter as Resident, to be more correct or more

* *Ante*, p. 35.   † Appendix B.   ‡ Appendix B.

conclusive than your last proceedings as Chief Commissioner. The report and receipt from the Committee nominated by Mr. Rungacharloo, accepted and forwarded by you, exactly constitute that mutual acquittance between Mr. Rungacharloo and yourself, which I foresaw would be proffered, and which I must still pronounce to be good for nothing. Under the circumstances already explained, the report of the Select Committee assembled by Mr. Rungacharloo in April 1881, is as worthless as that of the Select Committee assembled by you in November 1880, of which, indeed, it is a mere echo. One gentleman, Mr. Ananda Rao, who from his ability and official position must have taken the lead on the second occasion, was also on the former Committee. Your deputy, Colonel Hay, took part in both transactions.

The same deficiencies vitiate the two ostensible examinations, and render them equally illusory and futile as a release or acquittance between Ward and Guardian. There is no disinterested or independent party present. The whole question being one of value, there is no valuation. This last fatal defect, against which I raised, in good time, but in vain, a warning voice, is, also, noticed by Mr. P. Krishna Murti, the Jaghiredar of Yellandur and head of Poornia's family. "I am no judge", he says, "of the values, and no proper valuation was now taken."*

Perhaps he attached no particular meaning to those words when he placed them on record. Perhaps he had no particular doubt or misgiving when he revealed the two masked and unsecured doors.† I know nothing of this gentleman's capacity or strength of character, but the peculiarities of his position are sufficiently intelligible. He has probably felt himself helpless for some years; but, on the other hand, he alone among the seven signatories of your Report of November 1880, is rooted in Mysore by the enduring relations of ancestral fealty. Your official indemnities cannot absolve him. His honour and his house are pledged

---

* *Mysore Papers*, No. 1 of 1881, p. 173.   † *Ante*, p. 28.

to the Maharajah, and he may well wish them, and expect them, to outlast your incumbency and Mr. Rungacharloo's domination.

I do not believe, and no well-informed person believes, that these matters are definitively settled. Discussions and scandals of many years' currency, although they may be embittered, cannot be closed or dispelled by a dictatorial decree, but only by fair and open investigation. Though silence may seem to prevail in Mysore, the scandal subsists in full force. It may break out at any time,—the later the worse,—but its propagation in the dark, and in an aggravated form, must be even more injurious to Imperial authority. These considerations alone would sufficiently justify my persistence, and acquit me of any mischievous or malevolent object. My political purpose, however, is more complex and of wider extent.

I have resented—not unnaturally or unreasonably, I think—your imputations on my good faith; I have defended myself against them, not, I trust, ineffectually. But there never has been any malice or malevolence in my heart against you; while I entered on the inquiry, which led to my writing the Memorandum of 1880, signed "E. B.", with a positive prejudice in favour of Mr. Rungacharloo.

Almost the only act that seems to have seriously shaken his official credit and prospects, and brought down upon him, I believe, a reprimand, I was inclined to consider as a proof at once of his judgment and of his public spirit. Mr. L. B. Bowring, who, as that gentleman himself complained in a letter published in the *Bangalore Spectator*, dated "Torquay, 8th July 1874", "nominated him to the post of Controller", and was thereby "brought into an unfortunate collision with his superior", Colonel Haines,* had not long retired from the post of Chief Commissioner, before Mr. Rungacharloo, disguised as "a Native of Mysore", made an anonymous attack on his patron, accusing him of "a narrow policy" and of "a want of regard for the con-

* *Ante*, p. 6.

venience of the people". There was so much in this pamphlet* identical with my contention that nearly all the superfine changes in the administration of Mysore since General Cubbon's time have been changes for the worse,† that I did not feel at all inclined to find fault with Mr. Rungacharloo for what Mr. Bowring, in the letter already quoted, indignantly called "kicking down the ladder by which he rose". Mr. Rungacharloo seems, however, to have made a practice of thus kicking down ladders. I have become acquainted with his furtive detractions of Colonel Elliot and Colonel Malleson; I have been struck with his constant plan of submissively lurking behind each nominal superior in succession while present, and reviling him confidentially when absent or out of place. But until my attention was drawn to the matter now before us, I was disposed to think highly of Mr. Rungacharloo. The consistency with which I have always upheld the eligibility of natives of India for the very highest offices in their own country, might, I should hope, gain credit for the declaration that I have most reluctantly, in this instance, impugned the merits of an Indian who has attained an eminent position.

Leaving out of consideration, however, those matters of the Wardrobe and Jewel-room which, I maintain, have been unaccountably slurred over, Mr. Rungacharloo has attained this eminent position by means of some of the worst points in our system of Indian administration. Not being "a Native of Mysore", having no weight or influence by birth or connections, by character or conduct, either in the Palace or among the people,—being, in fact, an object of general distrust and dislike,—he has been forced on the reconstituted State as Minister, when he is known throughout Mysore simply as your man. The Maharajah has had no choice in the matter. The Imperial Government has not, either in the person of the Viceroy or of the Secretary of State, had any real voice or share in the

* *British Administration of Mysore*, Longmans, 1874.
† *Ante*, p. 5.

appointment. The over-centralisation at Calcutta defeats itself. Efficient control by the Viceroy in Council has become impossible. Each provincial authority who has the knack of keeping his files clear and his connection with "the Office" close, and who can give a good account of himself in an Administration Report, is, for his day, sole autocrat. He tells his own story, and there is no one to question it. Everything of consequence that goes to head-quarters is private and confidential; and many an important matter is settled by unrecorded notes or a quiet talk, before the form is gone through of taking the orders of Government. In all this, and in every instance, the public opinion of a province,—better informed always, and in time of need far more important, than any official opinion,—is inarticulate and inaudible.

Ever since I took to writing on Indian affairs I have preached one doctrine; and my single "political purpose" has been to make that doctrine understood and accepted by my fellow-countrymen. My doctrine is that India can only be kept under British supremacy, with any prospect of permanence and peace, as an Empire of confederated States and provinces, and not as a centralised Kingdom.

The policy proposed by Mr. Bright, in his great speech of the 24th of June 1858, on the second reading of the India Bill,—of breaking up the Empire into at least five independent Presidencies, defined in general by differences of language and geographical position—still shadows forth the only true policy in the stage at which we have arrived, for promoting the stability of the Empire and the peaceful progress of India. Mr. Bright's plan of decentralisation—a plan as sound and as practicable now as in 1858—was a statesmanlike protest against the vain attempt at governing two hundred millions of people, "twenty nations, speaking twenty languages," by means of a compact and centralised bureaucracy. If logically carried out,—liberalised, as we may be sure he would approve, by a wise and generous confidence in our own consultative and re-

E

presentative principles, and by an equitable admission of qualified Natives to the highest posts,— it might go a long way at least towards solving the almost insolvable problem of making our direct administration popular. "The essential problem of Indian statesmanship", as I have said elsewhere, "is how to reconcile self-government for India with Imperial supremacy for Great Britain. The true solution is that the more we concede the former, the more we confirm the latter."

At present, however, it is only in a reformed Native State that the possession of local self-government and submission to Imperial supremacy, can be completely reconciled. The most efficacious method of decentralisation,—efficacious at once for the financial relief and the moral reinforcement of the Paramount Power,— would be that of contracting the territories under our direct rule, reinstating and extending native administration in reformed and protected States. We could then greatly reduce our civil and military establishments. We could shift the burden of debt in great part from the Imperial Power to the allied Princes, by the legitimate and irresistible temptation of territorial aggrandisement.

Our direct administration has not as yet certainly become popular with any class, or in any locality. The divergence of feeling and interest between our people, official and non-official, and the Natives in our Provinces, is not an evil that tends to decrease or to cure itself. The Princes, on the other hand, fully appreciate the solid advantages of British Imperial supremacy. Our Commissioners and Collectors have no social influence, because they have no social intercourse with the people. But our Government is in close enough contact, and can keep up a clear enough understanding with the Indian Sovereigns and Chieftains through whom, if the practice of its "Political" representatives were so prescribed and so circumscribed as to be congenial and encouraging, it could govern and guide all the nations of India, and make Imperial supremacy popular. In proportion as we destroy, weaken, or alienate these manageable conservative powers, we shall stimulate and set loose the unmanageable brute force and fanaticism over which we have no control or influence whatever.

With these convictions and on these grounds, my course, however obscure, has been at least consistent. Before the great rebellion of 1857 opened the eyes of so many statesmen to the true conditions of our Indian Empire, my feeble voice had raised its petty protest, officially recorded, under peculiar circumstances, in a then recently annexed province, against the policy of annexation.

Before helping Colonel Macqueen and Dr. Campbell in London to counteract the importunate applications from Calcutta for the annexation of Mysore, I had, at Madras in 1861, recommended the very process of maintaining the State under an adopted heir, and of gradually restoring Native agency,* decreed by Lord Cranborne (now Marquis of Salisbury) and Sir Stafford Northcote in 1867, protracted and perverted by your predecessors and yourself.

Even with a Dewan of distinction, of good report and marked capacity, it would be no easy task now to "restore to the Maharajah the powers of government",† or to reconstitute Mysore as a substantive State, which were the professed objects of the statesmen of 1867, and of all their successors. With the Dewan you have set up, whose antecedents and public repute are such as I have indicated in this Letter, the task is an impossible one.

This is what attracts me, in pursuance of my "political purpose", to the situation in Mysore, even more than the unjustly discharged Sheristadar's personal appeal to me for help, or your charges against me of "garbling documents", "mischievous invention", and "weaving a malicious story". The whole course of Anglo-Indian official dealings with Mysore,—from the

* *Empire in India* (Trübner, 1864), pp. 304 to 316, 338 to 342, and 384 to 402.
† *Mysore Papers*, 385 of 1878, p. 135.

unwarranted sequestration in 1832, through forty years of constantly growing jobbery, and a strange period of heedless unconcern as to the evaporation of our Ward's valuables,—threatens to lead up to an apparent failure of the policy of reforming decentralisation in this recent and conspicuous essay. Believing the decided and systematic adoption of that policy, as a new departure in Imperial rule, to be the most efficient, if not the only remedy for the costliness and contemptuousness of our direct administration, I can only contemplate such an apparent failure as a disastrous probability. I might say much as to the means of yet averting it, but to those who are convinced of the disease the first measures for its cure are obvious enough.

After all, but for your mention of "a political purpose", as an aggravation of my "malicious story", I should hardly have been justified in extending so far the topics of this Letter. In the Memorandum of "E. B." I called for an independent examination and revaluation of the Mysore jewels. I have now endeavoured to show that my suggestion was well founded, and that such a scrutiny, if it has not by this time become impossible, is still much to be desired. I have endeavoured, also, to clear myself from those charges of malicious and mischievous misrepresentation which you have ventured to make against me, and which, as yet, you have entirely failed to justify.

   I have the honour to be,
    Your most obedient servant,
      EVANS BELL.

APPENDIX.

(A.)

In the latter part of 1874, the Chief Commissioner of Mysore, Sir Richard Meade, had before him the record of a trial in the preceding month before Major Hill, the District Magistrate of Mysore, of certain persons charged with being concerned in a "burglary" at the Mysore Palace, and he passed the following "Order thereon":—

No. 135.

"BANGALORE, 30th Nov. 1874.

"From the proceedings in the Magistrate's Court, it would appear that at least two burglaries were committed in the Maharajah's Palace at Mysore. The first seems from the evidence to have occurred in June 1872, when Mr. Vardon, the Police Inspector, drew the attention of Mr. Rungacharlu, the Controller of the Palace, to the rumour prevailing in the bazaar to the effect that certain valuable cloths had been stolen from the Jagan Mahal in the Palace. Mr. Rungacharlu thereupon inspected the room in which the property was kept, and found one of the iron bars of the window loose. This circumstance, however, raised little or no suspicion in his mind, and he merely ordered that the bar should be re-fastened.

"2. The second robbery took place early in May 1874. Soon afterwards, on inspection of the store-room, Mr. Rungacharlu discovered that a number of cloths were missing, and noticed that two of the iron bars in the same window were loose. Being then on the eve of proceeding to the Neelghiries on duty, he deferred taking any action till his return a fortnight after, merely ordering that the bars should be refastened, and private inquiries instituted in the matter. On the 17th of June, after examining five of the boxes containing the more valuable clothes, he found a large number missing, and then gave information to the Police, which resulted in the detection and conviction of the principal culprits. The number of cloths stolen was 234, and their cost is estimated at Rs. 49,080. Of these, 71 cloths, valued at Rs. 12,970, have been recovered, the actual loss is, therefore, estimated at Rs. 36,110.

"3. On the first occasion the action taken by the Controller was altogether inadequate. The boxes containing the valuable property kept in the store-room ought to have been at once carefully examined, and their contents checked with the original lists. Not only was this obvious and simple measure neglected, but the repair of the window-bar was executed in an inefficient manner.

"4. On the occasion of the second robbery, the condition of the window-bars ought at once to have satisfied Mr. Rungacharlu, as to the reality of the theft and the *modus operandi* of the thieves.

"Nevertheless, no attempt to ascertain the condition of the property was made, and no action beyond the measure, that had already proved futile, of re-fastening the bars, until the 17th of June, or nearly a month and a half afterwards, when some of the chests were examined, and cloths found missing. The Chief Commissioner notices that the evidence of the carpenters and other witnesses, who have deposed to the condition in which the bars were found, differs from that of the Controller, and indicates that due attention was not given by that officer to this most important of all the suspicious circumstances to which his attention has been called.

"5. It is, in fact, almost impossible to understand why so obviously serious a matter was, until the 17th of June last, dealt with so supinely. The slightest indication of anything suspicious in the state of the windows of a room containing property of such value ought, when coupled with the rumour which the Inspector brought to the notice of the Controller, to have been made the subject of prompt and full inquiry.

"6. It is clear that there is a want of system in the arrangements for the security of the very valuable property kept in the Palace. The Chief Commissioner requests that in future a formal examination of such property may be made every year, between the 1st of January and the 31st of March, under the superintendence of the Guardian. A report of the result should be submitted to this office. Where the property is packed in boxes, duly sealed and labelled, with a list of the contents, and which have not been opened, and are in proper condition, it will be sufficient to notice the fact.

"7. In order that reference may be made to them if necessary, the Chief Commissioner requests that copies of the lists of the property in question, prepared in 1868, may be furnished for record in this office, any changes that have taken place being duly noted in them.

"Ordered that a copy of these proceedings be submitted to the Government of India in the Foreign Department.

"(Sd.) H. WELLESLEY, *Offg. Secretary.*"

Evidently the Chief Commissioner and his Secretary had heard nothing of the "fresh lists" made in 1872, or of the "numerous inaccuracies" then found in the lists "prepared in 1868".

They seem to have taken things rather coolly in Mysore. According to the evidence given by Mr. Vardon, Inspector of Police, on the 12th September 1874, at the trial of the alleged burglaries of "the second occasion", Mr. Rungacharloo did on "the first occasion", in June 1872, examine the store-room, although the fact of the robbery, which undoubtedly had been perpetrated, seems not to have commended itself to his judgment. This is the substance of Mr. Vardon's testimony:—

"I told Mr. Rungacharloo my suspicions about two years ago, regarding the abstraction of cloths from the palace storeroom, and their being hooked out through the window. Mr. Rungacharloo said he did not believe it, as he kept the keys, but would go and see. I met him a few hours afterwards, and he told me my information was incorrect, and that no cloth were missing, but that an iron bar was loose. He quite disarmed my suspicions, and I made no further inquiry. I do not think I reported the matter to the Town Magistrate."

The Police Inspector makes no report of a "burglary" in the Palace to the Town Magistrate. The Controller of the Household and the Acting Guardian, Mr. J. D. Gordon, apparently make no report to anybody. The Chief Commissioner of Mysore in 1872, is left in blissful ignorance of the Wardrobe being robbed in June, and without any official report of the Jewelroom being opened in July for a six weeks' manipulation. He is neither informed that the strong-room has been found to be insecure, nor that the catalogue of "the very valuable property kept in the Palace" has been found to be very inaccurate. In consequence of a judicial inquiry in 1874, the "burglaries" in the Wardrobe and the laxity of "system in the arrangements", became incidentally known to the Chief Commissioner, but it is not until 1877 that another Chief Commissioner quite accidentally hears of the discrepancies and deficiencies in the Jewelroom, and of the unsanctioned and unreported operations of 1872, whereby the arrangements and lists of 1868, for which Major Elliot and Mr. Rungacharloo had received the thanks of Government, had been discredited, and discarded, in favour of a new arrangement and "fresh lists", by Mr. Gordon, without any official report.

In November 1874, however, the Chief Commissioner is roused to a sense that the "action" of Mr. Rungacharloo on "the first occasion" was "inadequate", and that "the valuable property kept in the store-room ought to have been at once carefully examined", and he directs an examination of "the very valuable property kept in the Palace" to be carried out between the 1st of January and the 31st of March in every year, "under the superintendence of the Guardian". A very striking proof of the loose discipline and inattention to the enforcement of orders which prevailed in this department of the Mysore administration is to be found in the fact that the examination thus ordered was never once instituted between November 1874 and October 1880. The Guardian, prompted by Mr. Rungacharloo, at once objected to this new scrutiny. The Chief Commissioner insisted, but his reiterated orders were of no effect.

The following correspondence was published, by direction or permission of the Chief Commissioner, in the Bangalore newspapers of the 14th of October 1880, after the Governor-General in Council had pronounced that Mr. Gordon's explanation in reply to the Memorandum signed " E.B.", was " completely satisfactory ".*

The Bangalore paper, in which I saw the letters, introduced them with these words of acknowledgment:—

"The following official papers about the property of the Mysore Palace have been kindly placed at our disposal."

No. 63.

" GUARDIAN'S OFFICE, MYSORE, *Dated* 22*nd December* 1874.

" *To the* SECRETARY TO THE CHIEF COMMISSIONER OF MYSORE.

" SIR,—With reference to the proceedings of the Chief Commissioner dated 30th November 1874, No. 135, I have the honour to forward herewith a Memorandum from the Controller giving an explanation of the circumstances connected with the robbery of clothes in the Palace, and trust that a perusal of the same may satisfy the Chief Commissioner that the action of the Controller, however it may appear in the light of subsequent discoveries, was in accordance with the view which the actual circumstances of the time justified his taking.

" 2. With regard to the arrangements existing for the security of the Palace property, I beg to state that the property in question consists of, firstly, jewellery, which are deposited in a room the key of which is held by me, and which is only opened in the presence of myself and that of the Controller. Secondly, of clothes which are perishable articles expended from time to time at the request of the Ranees, or for purposes connected with the Palace. The key of this room has been always in the custody of the Controller, in consequence of the necessity of frequently taking out cloths for Palace purposes. This room is opened only in the presence of the Controller with a number of Departmental Officers and a Sepoy guard; Thirdly, some jewellery belonging to the Chamundy Totty, or religious department, the key of which is also held by the Controller; and, Fourthly, of articles of jewellery, etc., in daily use of the several departments, which are necessarily left in their charge, subject to periodical examinations by the Controller. Lists of all this property, inclusive of the cloths, were prepared in 1868, and were forwarded to the Chief Commissioner's Office, and all subsequent changes of them are duly recorded in books kept in duplicate, one copy of which is kept with the Palace Officer and the other forwarded to the Guardian's office for record. I may add that changes in the jewellery can only take

---

* *Mysore Papers*, No. 1 of 1881, p. 150.

place with the sanction of the Chief Commissioner, which is duly recorded.

"With regard to periodical examinations of these properties, I may state that such are made of those in the hands of subordinate officers. But the examination of the great bulk of jewellery and cloths would require a very lengthened time, and may seem unnecessary so long as the key of the jewellery-room is held by me, and for which myself and the Controller are jointly responsible, and that of the cloth-room by him, and for which he is responsible, besides the regular Police Establishments, who look to the security of the room from day to day and keep their accounts. After the first preparation of the lists by Major Elliot, in 1868, an examination of the jewellery was made by Mr. Gordon, when he was officiating Guardian, in conjunction with the Controller, for the purpose of re-arranging them. It occupied nearly two months, and the accuracy of the original lists and the care with which these rooms have always been opened on subsequent occasions, have been remarkably proved by the absence of even a single error in the whole of this complicated property. Such examinations, I need hardly add, cannot be resorted to frequently with due regard to other work on hand, though it may sometimes be made with advantage, and I have only to assure the Chief Commissioner that every attention is bestowed on the careful preservation of the property and the proper keeping of the accounts.

" I have, etc.,
" (Sd.)   G. B. MALLESON,
" *Guardian to H. H. the Maharajah of Mysore.*"

[*Enclosure in the above.*]

MEMORANDUM.

" The Proceedings of the Chief Commissioner, dated 30th November 1874, No. 135, place the circumstances of the robbery of cloths in the Palace in such a light that I deem some explanation from me on the subject necessary, and I beg to submit the same.

" 2. These Proceedings seem to be based on the judgment recorded by the District Magistrate on the case. But the inquiry before that officer being only directed to the trial and conviction of the prisoners brought before him, any explanation of my action in the case can hardly find a place in it.

" 3. First, with regard to the robbery of June 1872, I beg to state that both myself and the Police Inspector, Mr. Vardon, were at the time engaged in endeavouring to trace out the perpetrators of the Treasury Robbery. Many persons were arrested and many houses were searched without any success. In the course of this inquiry, Mr. Vardon stated to me that he heard it mentioned that people were in the habit of drawing and taking away, by hooked sticks through the windows, cloths which were hung on the ropes in the Gagan Mahal. I was able to tell him at once that though cloths used to be so hung in the late Maharajah's days, they were all now in boxes, and that the report, like several others of the kind, was probably invented by those apprehended in the Treasury Robbery case, to put us on a wrong scent. I, however, thought it proper to open and examine the room, and found, as I expected, no cloths hung on ropes. My attention was necessarily drawn to the possibility of any access to the room, and neither myself nor the departmental officers who were all then with me could think of any. I noticed an iron bar in one of the skylight windows of the room was wanting, and I gave orders to the department concerned to have a new one fixed. There was nothing, however, in the circumstances to lead to any suspicion, as the building was old, and the possibility of any access through such narrow windows, thirty or forty feet from the ground, in a room situated in the middle of the zenana, and within reach of two guards, and in the vicinity of the cattle sheds, where several servants, who were considered to be generally of good conduct, always slept in the night, did not occur to my mind nor to the several officers of experience who were then with me. That the Inspector took no further notice of the matter, which, indeed, altogether passed out of his mind, would show what he then thought of the report, and it was only during my last inquiry that the circumstances brought to light seemed to confirm the old reports, and I myself brought it to notice.

" 4. On the second occasion I received a vague anonymous petition charging the Karohutty servants with the theft of cloths. False petitions of this description have always been numerous. Horses were posted for the Maharajah, and I had to start at once for Ootacamund. But I examined the room, found the bars in the window originally repaired loose, which was to be attributed to the imperfect manner in which the repair was made, or to actual theft. I examined one of the boxes containing the more valuable cloths, which seemed to contain a smaller number than usual. But, as cloths were expended out of the box, the exact state of things could only be found by examining the accounts. There was a suspicion of the robbery, and whilst I could not postpone my journey or leave the key of the room in any other hands, I made every adequate arrangement for the necessary preparation of the accounts for my further examination after my return, for placing additional guards in that part of the Palace, and, what seemed to be most important of all, for watching the suspected individuals. I returned about the 20th of May, and immediately set to work. The accounts of the expenditure of cloths, which were regularly kept in a book, had to be cast up in order to deduct the same from the original list, and, with the accounts thus prepared, I set myself to the examination of the 102 boxes in the room, which necessarily occupied several days. The Guardian having also returned, I communicated with him, and also gave information to the Magistrate and the Police Inspector. I must here explain that, owing to the failure of the measures taken by the Police to trace the perpetrators of the Treasury Robbery, I was inclined to trust very much to myself in the present case, and was especially anxious to avoid any needless display which might put the perpetrators on their guard. That, altogether, my plans were well concerted, and that, so far from being 'supine', my days and nights were anxiously devoted to the subject, would be seen from the fact that whilst the Police were not able to make any discovery from the 17th June, when they had information, to the 28th July, my exertions were crowned with success. I succeeded in tracing out the perpetrators of the robbery, the full information which I obtained led to some of them confessing, and indications of the houses in which the stolen cloths were deposited, were also obtained. I placed the particulars of the information I obtained before the Magistrate, the confessions were taken down, the suspected houses were searched, and a considerable number of valuable cloths, with Palace marks, were found; and thus, in the course of a single day, the perpetrators were apprehended, with such complete evidence as rendered their escape hopeless. I then left it to the Police to discover the other cloths from the information given by the prisoners, which they did successfully, in communication with me. I may thus state, without intending any disparagement of the efforts of the Police, that the discovery of the robbery in this instance was entirely the result of my exertions and the measures which I adopted.* Whilst I deeply deplored an event which could not have been foreseen by me, and, when dispassionately looked into, could only be regarded as a misfortune, I hoped that my exertions for the discovery of the robbery would contribute to remove any discredit to the department resulting from it.

"5. As regards the arrangements existing for the security of property in the Palace, they were carefully made by Major Elliot and approved of by his successors, and I am not aware that any improvement could be made in them. If any further instructions are given on the subject, they will be obeyed.

"(Sd.) C. RUNGACHARLOO,
"*Controller of H. H. the Maharajah's Household.*
" Dated 22nd December 1874."

No. 164.

" MYSORE CHIEF COMMR.'S OFFICE, CAMP PALLIEM,
" 11*th Jan.* 1875, *Residency Department.*

" *To the* GUARDIAN TO H. H. THE MAHARAJAH.

" SIR,—I am directed to acknowledge the receipt of your letter, dated the 22nd December 1874, forwarding a memo. from the Controller giving an explanation of the circumstances connected with the robbery of cloths in the Palace, and offering certain remarks in connection therewith.

---

* A very remarkable fact indeed. Mr. Rungacharloo traced and recovered some of the stolen goods when the Police were quite at fault.

"2. In reply, I am to state that the view taken by the Chief Commissioner in this case, as recorded in the order dated 30th November 1874, referred to by you, was formed on the Judicial Proceedings of the District Magistrate who investigated it, and which was transmitted by you as containing full particulars of the circumstances of the robbery, and without any comment on its statements. As you had been called on for a full report of these circumstances, it was naturally concluded that the account of the facts given in the said Proceeding was in all respects complete and satisfactory, and it is to be regretted that the further explanation now submitted was not forwarded with it, as the cause of the Controller's apparent inaction when the second robbery came to his notice, which was commented on in the order of 30th ultimo, is to some extent satisfactorily accounted for now; and the Chief Commissioner considers that the Controller is entitled to be relieved to some extent from the imputation of supineness to which he previously appeared to be fairly open.

"3. There is, however, I am to remark, one point in this explanation calling for notice, viz., that the looseness of the bars of the window, found by Mr. Rungacharloo on his examinination of the room on that occasion, was attributed by him to the imperfect manner in which the previous repairs had been made. It seems to the Chief Commissioner that this would have been impossible if—as ought to have been the case—a duly responsible person had superintended the repairs. With a ledge below the window, and the opposite house only three feet across, the perfect security of the windows should have been most jealously guarded, and there can be no question that from inadvertence this was not the case.

"4. From what has recently come to the Chief Commissioner's knowledge in connection with this case, it appears that the most valuable of the cloths are very rarely issued for use, and he thinks that they should be packed in secure boxes separately by themselves, which would admit of their being dealt with similarly to the jewels.

"5. It is not, of course, desired to give any unnecessary trouble in carrying out a periodical examination of the Palace valuables, in respect to which you may make such arrangements as you may deem most suitable and adequate. But an annual report of their security and general condition appears, to Sir Richard Meade, to be necessary, and he requests that a report may accordingly be made on 1st April 1875, as previously directed.

"I have, etc.,
"(Signed) H. W. WELLESLEY,
"*Offg. Secretary.*"

If Colonel Malleson, who, instructed by his ministerial subordinate, Mr. Rungacharloo, had just testified to the perfect accuracy of the original catalogue, had carried out Sir Richard Meade's reiterated orders, he must soon have ascertained some of the "great number of inaccuracies", and anticipated by nearly three years the partial disclosures of 1877. But Sir Richard

Meade's orders were not carried out, notwithstanding Mr. Rungacharloo's assurances that all "instructions" should "be obeyed".

No report was made on 1st April 1875, or in any subsequent year.

(B.)

"No. 673 I.P.

"*From* SIR A. LYALL, K.C.B., *Secretary to the Government of India,*
" *To* MAJOR EVANS BELL, LONDON.

" FOREIGN DEPARTMENT, *dated Simla, the* 26*th August* 1881.
" (Political.)

"SIR,—I am directed to acknowledge the receipt of your letters, dated respectively the 26th November and 17th December 1880, regarding the Mysore State Jewels.

["*From* ASSISTANT TO THE RESIDENT IN MYSORE,
" *No.* 8, *dated* 23*rd April* 1881,
" *To* RESIDENT IN MYSORE,
" *No.* 463, I.P., *dated* 26*th May* 1881.]

" 2. In reply, I am to forward, for your information, copy of the correspondence marginally noted, which has reference on the subject.

" I have the honour to be, Sir,
" Your most obedient servant,
" A. C. LYALL,
" *Secretary to the Government of India.*

" No. 8 (CAMP), *dated Ootacamund* 23*rd April* 1881.
" (Confidential.)

" *From*—W. J. CUNINGHAM, Esq., Bo.C.S., *Assistant to the Resident in Mysore,*

" *To*—A. C. LYALL, Esq., C.B., *Secretary to the Govt. of India, Foreign Dept., Simla.*

" I am directed by the Resident to forward, for the information of His Excellency the Viceroy and Governor-General in Council, copies of the receipt granted in acknowledgment of having received charge of the Mysore Palace jewels by the officers appointed for the purpose by His Highness the Maharajah, and of their report to His Highness.

" 2. It seemed to the Resident, I am to explain, to be expedient, with regard to certain statements recently made, and to the inquiries which had been instituted into the safety of the jewels, that special steps should now be taken for delivering and receiving charge of these jewels, with the utmost care and precision, and he requested that suitable arrangements should be made for doing so, and accordingly His Highness appointed the undermentioned officers to go through the lists of jewels, examine the jewels themselves, and, if found correct, to give an acquittance for them to Colonel A. C. Hay, late Commissioner of the Ashtagram Division, the officer who, under the directions of the Chief Commissioner, had immediate charge of them.

" 3. The officers were Bukshee Basavappajee Urs, Bukshee Viraraja Urs, Bukshee Nunjaraja Urs, P. Krishna Row Rai Bahadur, A. R. Sabanputty Mudaliar Rai Bahadur, and T. Ananda Row. The three first are His Highness's relations and principal officials in the Palace, the two next following are members of the recently-formed Council of His Highness the Maharajah, and the last is the officer who has been in joint charge of the Palace establishments and jewels.

" 4. The nomination of these officers appeared to Mr. Gordon to be perfectly suitable, and the result of their careful examination has been quite satisfactory, entirely corroborating, as it does, the result of the special inquiry made in October last under Mr. Gordon's personal supervision, which was duly reported to the Government of India."

"Having, by Memorandum No. 1, dated 6th instant, from the Dewan of Mysore,* been appointed by His Highness the Maharajah to take over charge of the Palace jewels hitherto placed, under the orders of the Chief Commissioner of Mysore, in charge of Colonel A. C. Hay, Commissioner of the Ashtagram Division, and Assistant Commissioner Mr. Ananda Row, in charge of Palace duties, and to give an acquittance to the officers of the British Government referred to, we have examined the said jewels and have submitted a report to His Highness the Maharajah, copy of which we subjoin, in which we state that we found all the jewels enumerated in Colonel Elliot's list, with the exception of those otherwise accounted for, to be forthcoming as described in the report of Mr. Gordon and other officers in December 1880, which we found to be correct in every particular; and we hereby acknowledge that we have received and taken charge of the said jewels, with the keys of the jewel-room, the locks of which have been secured under the seals of Bukshee Basavappajee Urs and P. Krishna Row, Esq., Rai Bahadur, one of His Highness's Councillors.

" (Sd.) BUKSHEE BASAVAPPAJEE URS.
,, BUKSHEE VIRARAJA URS.
,, BUKSHEE NUNJARAJA URS.
,, P. KRISHNA ROW.
,, A. R. SABANPUTTY MUDALIAR.
,, T. ANANDA ROW.

"Mysore, 18th April 1881."

---

* Mr. C. Rungacharloo.

"*Dated Mysore, 18th April* 1881.

"*From*—BUKSHEE BASAVAPPAJEE URS and five others,
"*To*—HIS HIGHNESS THE MAHARAJAH OF MYSORE.

"We, the undersigned, beg respectfully to submit that, in pursuance of your Highness's instructions, conveyed through the Dewan, and the wishes of the British Resident, communicated by Colonel Hay, we proceeded to take an account of the Palace jewels in presence of that gentleman. The operation commenced on Saturday the 9th instant, and was concluded on Saturday the 16th.

"We took for our guide the original list of 1868, prepared under the orders of Colonel Elliot, and the Palace diaries, and went on examining jewel by jewel, noting down against each number any little variation in the number of precious stones, etc., that might be noticed. In cases of doubtful identity, we counted the most valuable precious stones in the jewel, and in a few instances had the article weighed, or the metal assayed as necessity arose, and were thus enabled satisfactorily to identify the whole of the jewels.

"Our task was greatly facilitated by the minute examination made by Mr. Gordon and other officers in October 1880, the report of which found to be correct in every particular, and by the excellent classification and arrangement of the jewels made by the Palace authorities.

"Feeling thus satisfied that all the jewels enumerated in Colonel Elliot's list, with the exception of those that are noted as being otherwise disposed of, or in Your Highness's own use, are forthcoming and are identical, we have taken over charge of the jewel-room, and put on an additional padlock, with our several seals affixed on it, pending further instructions, and have likewise given an acquittance to Colonel Hay, a copy of which we humbly submit for Your Highness's information."

"No. 463 I.P., *dated* SIMLA, 26*th May* 1881.

"*From*—SECRETARY TO THE GOVT. OF INDIA, Foreign Dept.,
"*To*—RESIDENT, Mysore.

"I am directed to acknowledge the receipt of your Assistant's letter No. 8 of the 23rd April 1881, regarding the transfer of the Palace jewels to His Highness the Maharajah.

"2. Having regard to the importance of the matter, you very properly arranged for a careful examination of the jewels, before transfer, by officers of the Mysore Durbar; and their report, enclosed in your letter, is entirely satisfactory. I am to say that your proceedings are approved by the Government of India."

"*From* MAJOR EVANS BELL,

"*To the* SECRETARY TO THE GOVERNMENT OF INDIA IN THE FOREIGN DEPARTMENT, CALCUTTA.

"110, HOLLAND ROAD, KENSINGTON, LONDON, W.

"*September* 30*th*, 1881.

"SIR,—I have the honour to acknowledge the receipt of your letter No. 673, I.P., dated the 26th of August 1881, enclosing for my information copy of a letter from the Assistant Resident in Mysore, dated the 23rd of April, and of a receipt and report signed by Basavappajee Urs and five others, dated the 18th of May last, relating to the transfer of the Mysore Palace jewels from the charge of certain British officers into the custody of the Maharajah's own servants. The Government of India, in a letter to the Resident in Mysore, No. 463, I.P., dated the 26th of May last, with a copy of which I am also furnished, pronounce the proceedings regarding this transfer to be entirely satisfactory.

" 2. The communication with which I have thus been honoured is made, you inform me, with reference to my letters dated respectively the 26th of November and the 17th of December 1880, with which I beg to be allowed to associate the Memorandum on the Mysore jewels, published with my initials, E. B., in the Calcutta *Statesman* on the 7th of April and 16th of June 1880.

" 3. That Memorandum, which was, of course, written in the hope of leading to some inquiry and to certain precautions, has already been noticed in the proceedings of the Government of India, No. 813, dated 25th December 1880, and in a despatch to the Secretary of State, No. 114, dated the 29th of December 1880, which are published in the Papers presented to Parliament, C 3026 of 1881.

" 4. I considered it my duty, in the last paragraph of that Memorandum, after pointing out what seemed to me to be grave reasons for an independent inquiry, to urge that 'if the very same functionaries who had been singled out by circumstances for sole responsibility, were to be left unprotected by any inquiry or supervision, to hand over to the young Maharajah, by their own method and process, property valued in 1868 at more than £350,000, and virtually to grant themselves an acquittance, the seed would be sown for future crops in mischievous rotation of incurable scandals and unanswerable claims'. I learn from the papers you have now forwarded to me, that the very course which I humbly ventured to deprecate has been pursued. No independent inquiry has been made; no precautions have been taken. Sir James Gordon, lately Chief Commissioner and Guardian, now Resident, and Mr. C. Rungacharloo, formerly Controller of the Household, now Dewan, have been left to effect the transfer by their own method and process, and have granted themselves a mutual acquittance.

"5. I considered it my duty in the last paragraph of my letter dated the 26th of November 1880, to remind the Government of India that the persons within the Mysore territory most deeply interested, and most fully informed as to the jewel affairs, as well as those who must be more or less implicated in any irregularities or malpractices, if any such had occurred, were either persons in authority, or under authority, either in a position to dominate, or liable to intimidation. I ventured, therefore, with great deference, to urge that any investigation guided and presided over by the local authorities in Mysore, must be delusive and inconclusive, and that the agency for such an investigation ought to be, as recommended by Captain F. A. Wilson in 1877, 'special', and, I added, of unquestionable independence. The papers published, and the papers now forwarded by you to me, show that no real investigation has been made; that such ostensible inquiries as have taken place have been guided and presided over by the local authorities; that the several Committees appointed to examine, transfer, and receive charge of, the Mysore jewels, have been selected by Sir James Gordon, as Chief Commissioner and Resident, and by Mr. C. Rungacharloo as Secretary and Dewan. Not only was the Committee assembled in October 1880 to examine the jewels composed of Mr. Gordon's own subordinates, but it was composed exclusively of officers who at one time or another had been partially in charge of the jewels. According to Sir James Gordon's own despatch of the 18th of December 1880, 'specific statements' having been made, he seriously announces to the Government of India that he has met the specific statements by combining all the persons whom they affect, more or less, into a Committee to give them a general contradiction.

"6. In the same letter, I ventured to urge on the Government of India that the main point for investigation being the actual present value of the jewels, as compared with the estimated value of 1868, a valuation was essential. I learn from the receipt and report appended to your letter to me, dated 18th April 1881, from Bukshee Basavappajee Urs, and five others, appointed by the Dewan, Mr. C. Rungacharloo, that no valuation of the jewels was made by them.

"Moreover, I learn from Enclosure No. 5 of the despatch from the Government of India to the Secretary of State, No. 114, dated the 29th of December 1880, that no valuation of the jewels was made by the Committee assembled under the guidance and control of Mr. Gordon and Mr. Rungacharloo at Mysore in 1880. Mr. P. N. Krishna Murti, Deputy-Commissioner, states, in answer to Question 7:—'I am no judge of the values, and no proper valuation was now taken.'

F

" 7. The Government of India not having judged it necessary or advisable to make any such inquiry, or to take any such precautions as I considered it my duty to suggest, before handing over charge of the Mysore jewels to the Maharajah, I do not conceive that it would be either useful or becoming for me to submit any further observations on the subject for the judgment of the Government of India.

" I have the honour to be, Sir,

" Your most obedient servant,

" EVANS BELL, Major,
" *Late of the Madras Staff Corps.*"

ADVERTISEMENT.

I have said at page 52 of this Letter that the sequestration of Mysore in 1832 was "unwarranted". That the sequestration of the State was not warranted, either from the subsidy being in arrears or in jeopardy, or by any other provision in the Treaty, or by the exigencies of the time, I shall prove clearly in

SOME WORDS AND WORK OF GENERAL JOHN BRIGGS,

which I hope to publish before the end of the year. I shall, also, show why, in the interests of the Empire, these facts ought to be understood and appreciated.

A LETTER TO H. M. DURAND, Esq., C.S.I., FROM MAJOR EVANS BELL.

A LETTER

TO

H. M. DURAND, Esq., C.S.I.,

OF THE BENGAL CIVIL SERVICE, BARRISTER-AT-LAW;

FROM

MAJOR EVANS BELL,

LATE OF THE MADRAS STAFF CORPS;

AUTHOR OF "LAST COUNSELS OF AN UNKNOWN COUNSELLOR", "THE OXUS AND THE INDUS",
"RETROSPECTS AND PROSPECTS OF INDIAN POLICY", ETC.

LONDON:
CHATTO AND WINDUS, PICCADILLY.

1884.

Price Two Shillings.

LONDON:
WHITING AND CO., LIMITED, SARDINIA STREET, LINCOLN'S-INN-FIELDS.

NOTICE.

I WISH to explain, in as few words as possible, that although the publication of this Letter is forced upon me by a personal attack, it is not merely to a personal controversy, or to a private grievance, that I ask public attention. I claim to represent the interests of the Empire in opposition to Mr. H. M. Durand, who champions the interests of a family, a class, and a profession.

A Prince of the Empire, marked out by the Imperial Government in 1858 as one of the intended recipients of "honorary distinctions" and "territorial grants", in reward for services rendered during the rebellion, has received no reward at all, and has, on the contrary, been treated with contumely and calumny. Against this treatment he has continuously protested, more especially since its renewal in 1870, but without obtaining redress.

The only Resident at a Native Court of any consequence who broke down completely in the crisis of 1857 was Colonel (afterwards Sir Henry) Durand, in charge of the Residency at Indore, Holkar's capital, during the absence of Sir Robert Hamilton. He was so blind as to what was passing close to his own doors; so neglectful of friendly intercourse with the Court and its notabilities; so arrogantly regardless of Native counsels and opinions, that a combined attack by mutineers in our service and in that of Holkar took him quite by surprise, forced him to leave the Residency, and to take refuge in the British station of Hoshungabad. Here he jumped to the conclusion that Holkar was implicated in the revolt; declared, in the style of Napoleon, "The dynasty of Holkar has ceased to reign", and denounced the Maharajah's "Mahratta treachery" in his despatches. But at that very time the Maharajah was co-operating most gallantly with the English gentlemen who had taken up Colonel Durand's duties during his unlucky retirement. Colonel Durand would give no credit to Holkar or to any of his own brother officers for what was done while he was absent from the scene. He ever afterwards acted as if any acknowledgment on his part of Holkar's good influence and services would leave his own failure and flight without excuse. Circumstances placed him for eleven years in a position to prevent any redress of the injustice done to the Maharajah. His Assistants and successors at Calcutta have always made common cause with him, as English officials generally incline to do where the appellant, even though he may be a Prince, is "only a Native". In the words of Sir John Kaye, the historian of the *Sepoy War*, "Holkar was sacrificed to Durand". I will add, and I will prove, that the authority, the dignity, and the honour of the Empire, have been sacrificed to sustain the interests and the credit of "the Office" and "the Service".

I will now give, in the most striking and succinct form that suggests itself to me, a brief hint and outline of the hitherto unequal contest that has been going on, in this matter, between

IMPERIAL INSTRUCTIONS AND OFFICIAL OBSTRUCTIONS.
1858-1860.

Lord Stanley (now Earl of Derby) President of the Board of Control, writes as follows (through the Secret Committee of the Court of Directors), on the 28th of July 1858, to the Governor-General:—

"We desire that you will, as expeditiously as possible, furnish us with a list of those Princes, Chiefs, and others, who have distinguished themselves by acts of fidelity and friendship to the British Government, together with a statement of their services, and of your views with respect to the best means of rewarding them, whether by territorial grants, by pensions or gratuities, or by honorary distinctions.

"The first of these modes would doubtless be the most acceptable to those whom we desire to gratify.

"High on the list you will, we feel assured, place the names of Scindia, HOLKAR, the Nizam, and the King of Nepaul."

In a despatch, dated 31st December 1858, Lord Stanley, Secretary of State for India, observes that he is waiting for a reply to the letter just quoted, and adds:

"I trust no long time will elapse before I receive from your Lordship further reports of the same kind, including the names of the more influential Princes of India, especially those of the Maharajahs Scindia and HOLKAR, and of his Highness the Nizam."

Territorial rewards were conferred upon "Scindia, the Nizam, and the King of Nepaul". But with regard to the fourth Prince, "high on the list" of those whom Her Majesty's Government "desired to gratify", the Viceroy, Lord Canning, in a despatch dated January 16th, 1860, wrote as follows:—

"It is not my intention to propose that his Highness" (the Maharajah HOLKAR) "should receive any gift of territory. His conduct on the day on which his troops mutinied and attacked the Residency at Indore was not such as to command either the respect or the gratitude of the British Government."

This dishonouring and insulting sentence was not preceded, accompanied, or followed by any justification or explanation.

1864.

Her Majesty's Government, having never been told why Holkar was blamed and unfavourably distinguished from the other Princes in the list, Sir John (now Lord) Lawrence, soon after his arrival as Viceroy at Calcutta, receives from Sir Charles Wood (now Lord Halifax), Secretary of State, a letter dated 4th of July 1864, inquiring why no reward had been conferred on the Maharajah HOLKAR, and asks for information from the "Office".

In answer to Sir John Lawrence's requisition, Colonel Durand, now Foreign Secretary to the Government of India, sends up a secret "Office-note", dated August 4th, 1864, to the Viceroy in Council, with these words:—

"HOLKAR has got all that Lord Canning thought he should get. He was, also, given the Star of India—why, no one could ever make out—and it deteriorated the value of the decoration in the eyes of those who, like the Begum of Bhopal, knew HOLKAR's conduct."

These remarks, as will be shown more fully and clearly in my Letter, are at once unmannerly and unmeaning. They were accompanied by no explanatory statement.

1870.

The Earl of Mayo, Viceroy of India, unable to account for HOLKAR's disgrace and forfeiture, asks for information from "the Office".

In answer to Lord Mayo's requisition, the Foreign Secretary, Mr. (now Sir Charles) Aitchison sends up a secret "Office-note", dated 5th August 1870, of which the following is an extract:—

"HOLKAR did not, at the first burst of the mutiny, take that open and decided part with us that he ought to have done. The attack upon the Indore Residency occurred on the 1st July 1857. It was not till the 5th that he took any decided steps to show with which cause he intended to throw in his lot."

"On the 5th of July the Maharajah, and not before, sent a deputation to Mhow to express his regret at what had occurred."

This was the first intelligible charge that had ever been made against the Maharajah Holkar, and it is entirely false. It has no foundation in any official report, and it is contradicted by official reports on record.

My lamented friend, John Dickinson, had occupied himself for years with Indian politics, as other men of large means and abundant leisure may take up horse-racing, numismatics, or entomology. He had a friendly correspondent, Captain Fenwick, in Holkar's service,* and thus became acquainted, from day to day, with all the incidents of the rebellion, and with all the perverse influences by which the Maharajah Holkar's character was maligned and his life embittered. Mr. Dickinson worked at the redress of this great wrong until his death, and left it as a legacy to me, previous arrangements having been made so that I should be enabled on occasion, and as opportunity offered, to give some time to the very unprofitable pursuit of what Mr. H. M. Durand would call "a hired advocate", or "a paid agitator".

I have tried, with my very modest appliances, and in my very obscure position, to fulfil to the utmost the responsibilities thus entailed upon me. I was really beginning to think that I had done my utmost, and that my responsibilities were drawing to a close. I was on the point of telling both appellant and judge that I had made my last effort, when Mr. H. M. Durand insists on a combat *à outrance* which I had hardly contemplated, and compels publicity being given to certain details which I had intended to keep in reserve. I cannot profess to regret this compulsion, either on private or on public grounds.

Since Mr. H. M. Durand has ventured to accuse me, without subverting, or, indeed, impugning, anything that I have written, of having published "a tissue of untruths", "a string of misstatements", I have placed in the British Museum a copy of a volume called *Holkar's Appeal*, containing all the documents and *pièces justificatives* quoted in the following pages, and in the *Last Counsels of an Unknown Counsellor*. I have placed another copy in the London Library, and have distributed a few more where attention is likely to be given to them.

E. B.

---

* See *Last Counsels of an Unknown Counsellor* (Macmillan, 1877), p. 20.

TO

H. M. DURAND, Esq., C.S.I.,

OF THE BENGAL CIVIL SERVICE, BARRISTER-AT-LAW;

Author of *Central India in 1857*,* and of the *Life of Sir Henry Marion Durand, K.C.S.I., C.B.*†

SIR,

On the best and latest authorities I find that you hold the place of Under-Secretary to the Government of India in the Foreign and Political Department, and that you held it in December, 1883, when you published the second work mentioned in the superscription of this letter. Those who have the best experience and opinion of your talents, will not deny that this early preferment was partly due to your father's professional and social connections. It would but be in accordance with Anglo-Indian tradition and precedent if you were to look forward to rising from the second to the highest place in that Office over which Sir Henry Durand presided for five years, and exercised considerable control for five subsequent years. That Secretaryship, you tell us, "has been, and is still, regarded as the blue riband of the Civil Service, is greatly coveted for its own sake, and is an almost certain stepping-stone to the highest posts in the Empire."‡ In the meantime you seem to have formed a sufficiently high estimate of your duties, and of the qualifications demanded for their fulfilment. At the beginning of the chapter in which you describe your father's tenure of that appointment, you observe that it

---

* Ridgway, Piccadilly, 1876; originally published as an article in the *Calcutta Review* for April, 1876.

† W. H. Allen, Waterloo Place, 1883.

‡ *Life of Sir Henry Durand*, vol. i, p. 282.

is "one of the most interesting and important in India. The control of our relations with the feudatory States of India, comprising one fourth of the entire continent, and containing a population of nearly sixty millions, is", as you very justly observe, "a weighty task, and requires much firmness and tact." "Such qualifications", you continue, "are rare, and they should be possessed by an Indian Foreign Secretary; for, as regards this important branch of our Indian policy, he is in fact the responsible adviser and right hand of the Viceroy." It is, indeed, as you remark, "hardly too much to say that, by the bulk of the Native Chiefs, his office is regarded as second in importance only to that of the Viceroy."*

Neither the question of your possessing the "rare qualifications" for this important office, nor that of your father having possessed them, would ever have been raised by me, had you not forced me to enter on them both by a very serious personal charge. You accuse me of having published a book which you declare to be "a tissue of untruth". The feeble style in which you deliver this poisoned and Parthian dart, in the very last paragraph of your Appendix, betrays a deficiency both in "tact" and in "firmness". The blow, as I shall prove, is a foul one and badly aimed. You say that the "attacks" upon your "father's character", on the subject of his treatment of the Maharajah Holkar, have been "shameless", "violent and acrimonious", and that "it would now be equally impossible and useless" to "avoid the controversy";† and yet you do avoid it. You did not answer my book, *Last Counsels of an Unknown Counsellor*, when it appeared, and you "do not purpose" to do so now—although its "refutation" would have been "clear and easy"—because you are "assured" it must "die a natural death". "Firmness" is decidedly wanting here.

There seems to me to be a want of "tact" in the use of offensive and provoking language without justifying its use by reason and evidence. If my book had really been a "violent and acrimonious tissue of untruth", "a

* Vol. i, pp. 280, 282. † Pp. 236, 476.

string of misstatements",* its refutation must have been to you, with all the records of Government, and all your father's papers, at your command, the most easy matter in the world. Yet you have not attempted it. There is neither "firmness" nor "tact" in calling Mr. Dickinson "a pamphleteer", or in making dark hints about "paid advocates" and "hired agitators", while you express a hope that the book, which you cannot answer, may "die a natural death". Such language is not, in any sense of the word, strong. It is at once evasive and abusive. Language is never truly strong, unless it is just. The charge, moreover, you bring against Mr. Dickinson and myself, of being "violent and acrimonious", is utterly unfounded. You are as incapable of justifying it as you are of justifying the more serious charge of "untruth" which, to adopt your language but not your tactics, I now find it "impossible to avoid". I do not intend to avoid it. Without imitating your acrimonious language, I retort that charge in substance upon you, and shall prove it up to the hilt.

The *Protest and Rejoinder* on behalf of the Maharajah Holkar, which formed the second portion of the *Last Counsels of an Unknown Counsellor*, is rightly called by you "the posthumous work of Mr. John Dickinson".† Had he lived, he would have been solely responsible for it, and my name, in all probability, would not have appeared at all. He was a wealthy and influential man, and I was his paid assistant. At his death I revised and published the book, a great part of which I had written. I then became alone responsible for what you venture to characterise as "a tissue of untruth". With my name on the title-page, and my statement that I had "for a long time been associated" with Mr. Dickinson in his work,‡ all this was obvious enough, and had been, also, made known to you by my private explanations when the book was published. Under these circumstances, I can see no "tact" in your affected aversion "to speak of Mr.

* P. 476. † *Life of Sir H. Durand*, vol. i, pp. 463, 476.
‡ *Last Counsels of an Unknown Counsellor* (Macmillan & Co., 1877), p. 59.

Dickinson in the tone which he", according to your complaint, "adopted towards your father and yourself",* while you insult him by impeaching his veracity. You make no attempt to justify that impeachment, because "Mr. Dickinson is dead", and because you are "assured" his posthumous work will "certainly die a natural death". I can see no "firmness" in this manœuvre to the rear. Your assurance was very ill-founded. The book is intact, and Mr. Dickinson's representative is alive.

You should have remembered that the book in question was a rejoinder to the pamphlets published by General Travers and yourself. You might have remarked a peculiar difference in the style with which I treated his pamphlet and yours. Notwithstanding his bitter prejudice against Holkar, blindly accepted from his personal friend, Colonel Durand, in General Travers I always recognised a chivalrous and gallant soldier, and a perfectly trustworthy informant as to matters that had fallen under his own observation. He is one of my most important witnesses, the more valuable because reluctant and hostile.

But I charged you with misstatements and exaggerations which could not easily be explained or excused even with the most liberal allowance for filial respect and affection. Your method of meeting this charge is peculiar. You will not answer my book, but you admit that you "have been accused of exaggerating".† You then maintain and repeat the exaggerations of your pamphlet in more vague and general terms, omitting the salient points that had made my exposure of your inaccuracy so effective and so conspicuous. For example, in the large volume you no longer say that your father "*saw* the whole of Holkar's troops surging up to surround the Residency".‡ Still, as they stand at present, the exaggerations, direct or suggested, are sufficiently remarkable in your later publication.

"The attack," you say, "was no longer a tentative one. Encouraged by the impunity with which the guns had

---

* Vol. i, p. 476.   † P. 467.   ‡ *Central India in* 1857, p. 55.

for nearly two hours cannonaded the Residency, Holkar's troops in the City came pouring up to their support."*

And then you go on to say that Holkar had " nine good English guns, 1,400 Cavalry and about 2,000 Infantry", and that " the lines were rapidly emptied "—just as if all these troops had appeared on the scene, or had made a threatening demonstration. Refusing to answer or notice my " violent and acrimonious" book, in the hope that it may " die a natural death", you remain obstinately silent as to the conclusive evidence therein adduced that no such demonstration was made. Dr. Charles Thomson, in medical charge, who was present during the attack, and accompanied Colonel Durand's retreat, in the written statement he made on the 22nd of January, 1858, says :—

" After having retired a very short distance from the Residency, the mutineers did not molest us, *and during the whole of the mutiny I never saw any of the mutineers.*"†

A fortiori, he never saw " Holkar's troops pouring up", " Cavalry, Infantry, and Artillery pouring up in a mass", " the whole of Holkar's troops surging up", " surging up to surround the Residency, masses of Holkar's troops, consisting of 1,400 Cavalry, 2,000 Infantry, and 25 to 30 guns, besides any amount of armed rabble from the city."‡

The unimpeachable evidence of your father's friend, General Travers, which I shall quote in a passage from your own book, proves likewise that neither he nor your father saw, or fancied they saw, any additional force of Holkar's troops from the City arriving to join in the attack on the Residency. This is what you say :—

" The overwhelming strength of the enemy's force on this occasion has never, I think, been fully realised. General Travers in his pamphlet speaks of the ' overwhelming numbers' against us; but he further describes the force as follows :—' Three field guns, one more or less damaged, nine or ten companies of Infantry,

---

* Vol. i, p. 215.
† Letter from Governor-General's Agent to Secretary in Foreign Department (General No. 309A), No. 47, 9th February, 1858 ; *Last Counsels*, p. 99.
‡ *Central India in* 1857, pp. 53, 54, 55.

and an increasing armed crowd from the City.' Similarly, Colonel Malleson writes of "six hundred trained Sepoys, swelled by the constantly augmenting rabble of the City."*

But where are the "nine good English guns, the 1,400 Cavalry, and the 2,000 Infantry", "surging up"? You do not give us the explanatory statement of Colonel Malleson, from the personal information of General Travers, that the force of "six hundred trained Sepoys" consisted of "about two hundred of all ranks of Holkar's men, and the Contingent Infantry"—our own Sepoys—"who just about this time fairly went over to the rebels." † There is nothing here as to "Holkar's troops from the City pouring up to their support".

Neither in his original military despatch, enclosed in Colonel Durand's letter to Government, dated Hoshungabad, 9th of July, 1857, nor in the equally modest and candid narrative of his exploit published in 1876, does General Travers speak of any assailants or opponents except the "Regular Infantry" and "three guns", "sent by the Maharajah Holkar for the protection of the Residency", and "an armed crowd from the direction of 'the City'." He never said one word as to any hostile Cavalry, additional guns, or troops of any description arriving or looming in the distance.

In describing the first incidents of the attack, you say that the guns "were supported by Holkar's Cavalry".‡ This is an utterly unfounded and unwarrantable misstatement, contradicted by the military despatch of Major Travers, as well as by the gallant General's published narrative of 1876. There is nothing to show that even as many as a dozen rebel horsemen were seen by anyone in addition to the "eight troopers" who, according to General Travers,§ accompanied Saadut Khan, and who doubtless were cowed by the dashing

---

* Vol. i, Appendix, pp. 466, 467.

† *Malleson's History of the Indian Mutiny*, vol. i (Allen, 1878), footnote to p. 224. See also General Travers' *Evacuation of Indore* (H. S. King & Co., 1876), pp. 9 and 56.

‡ P. 214.   § *Evacuation of Indore*, p. 12.

charge of the English Commandant, in which their leader was wounded.

You say, quite correctly, that "the force from the Residency retired at a walk".*

The party consisted of seventeen English persons, besides eight women and two children. General Travers says, " Our draught bullocks could not be forced beyond a rate of two and a half to three miles an hour."† If even a hundred horsemen—to say nothing of "masses" or "swarms pouring up"—had intervened or pursued, the whole party must have been massacred.

The gross and palpable exaggerations of your pamphlet, unretracted, but reproduced in a more shadowy form, in your large book, are not only unsupported but absolutely contradicted by the recorded statements of General Travers and of Sir Henry Durand. For example, Colonel Durand, writing to Lord Lovaine on September the 29th, 1857, speaks of "the humiliation of being forced to withdraw before an enemy that I despised, *and who, could I have got anything to fight, would have been easily beaten back.* As it was, with only fourteen Golundauz who would stand by their guns, we not only held our own for about a couple of hours, but beat back their guns, and gained temporary advantage. We retired unmolested in the face of superior masses."‡ Can anyone believe that Holkar's troops, "Cavalry, Infantry, and Artillery in a mass, with additional guns", "swarming", "surging", and "pouring up", could have been "easily beaten back" by Colonel Durand and his "fourteen Golundauz", or if he had seen them, would have been "despised"? Observe particularly that Colonel Durand says he was "*forced to withdraw* before" the "enemy he despised", not before "masses", whom he could not have despised, "swarming", "surging" or "pouring up". The "masses", the "swarms", the "Cavalry cutting off the retreat", existed only in the treacherous voices of our Mahidpore and Bhopal Sepoys, with whom the hasty and

---

* P. 471. † *Evacuation of Indore*, p. 16.
‡ Kaye's *Sepoy War*, vol. iii, pp. 332, 333 ; *Last Counsels*, p. 105.

half-pretended attack of Holkar's detachment was concerted.

The exaggerations in which you persist compel me to call attention to the true nature and proportions of the attack on the Indore Residency. You speak of the imaginary mass of Holkar's troops " pouring up from the City", having been " encouraged by the impunity with which the guns had for nearly two hours cannonaded the Residency."* More remarkable than " the impunity" of the cannonade was its ineffectiveness. Here is your own description of the Residency. It "was a stone building, standing in an open space, and pierced in the lower story by some five-and-twenty or thirty glass and venetian doors, incapable", according to Colonel Malleson, " of resisting even a kick."† " Holkar's guns", you say in another place, " had now moved round to their original position, where they had more shelter, and were pouring a well-directed fire of round shot and grape into the Residency building itself. This did little harm, beyond breaking a few panes of glass."‡

In this cannonade of two hours—" well directed," you say, for some time—a few panes of glass were broken, and only one of the English defenders, Sergeant Murphy, was wounded. " In the fight itself", you say, " our loss had not been heavy. A few Bhopal Contingent horsemen, a few Bheels and some bullocks were killed; and one of the European sergeants was wounded. These were the only casualties."§

The affair of the Indore Residency was, with the exception of the daring charge of Major Travers, entirely an artillery duel, in which all the skill, and probably all the real fighting, was on our side, and in which our side had the best of it; for while only one of the men with our guns was wounded, we disabled one of the enemy's guns, which is not likely to have occurred without some of the enemy being killed. It is not easy to understand how so many cannon-balls could fly about harmlessly; and you may be right in saying that " a few Bhopal horsemen, a

---

* P. 215.   † P. 466, footnote.   ‡ P. 215.   § P. 216.

few Bheels and some bullocks were killed". But there is much reason to believe that the assailants had no wish to hurt any of our Sepoys, with whom the outbreak was concerted. Colonel Durand, in his despatch of 13th August, 1857, says :—" There cannot be the slightest doubt that the attack on the Residency was concerted with the Bhopal and Malwa Contingents, and with the conspiracy of the Mhow troops."

It was in the fact that Major Travers did not know what he was charging that the gallantry of the deed which won him the Victoria Cross consisted. For all he knew, he was leading five troopers against three guns supported by a compact body of Infantry. He was really attacking a half hearted and bewildered body of mutineers, without a leader, without any object except that of plundering the Residency, and without any intention of coming to blows with their treacherous accomplices. Major Travers could only rally five of his men to follow him for five minutes. It was treachery, not physical cowardice, that kept his men back. The General himself, with that touching reluctance to abandon faith in his own men that was admirably but fatally conspicuous in so many instances during the mutinies, talked to the last of their " loyalty", and of distrust and panic among them. But there was no panic : there was, as you say, treason in their ranks. General Travers, in a passage which you quote,* states that when he tried to form the picket for his charge on the guns, the formation was three times broken from the rear by a native officer, who was afterwards hung for his misconduct.† It was, also, proved at the trial of Saadut Khan in 1874 that the rebel leader was accompanied at his parade on the 2nd of July, 1857, by several troopers of Major Travers' regiment.

The sole excuse for the false notions as to the origin and basis of the outbreak under which Colonel Durand left the Residency, and made his first reports to Bombay and to Calcutta, is to be found in the lies that were told to Major Travers by his treacherous troopers, with the

---

* P. 213.   † *Evacuation of Indore*, p. 13.

obvious intention of hastening the evacuation of the Residency, and leaving it clear for plunder. "On the field at Indore", says General Travers, "one of my Sepoys (Gunesh Singh, I think), told me that the Maharajah had ordered the attack",—that "most of the Sepoys had heard the order given, and that it had turned many against us."* This was a malignant lie, but it led Colonel Durand at once to commit himself in his notes to the Commandant of Mhow, and in his early correspondence with Lord Elphinstone and Lord Canning, to the assertion that they were "attacked by Holkar" "with true Mahratta treachery".

Major Travers, again, in paragraph 5 of his military despatch, enclosed in Colonel Durand's letter from Hoshungabad of the 9th of July, 1857, says:—"I was led to believe by reports from my Cavalry that our left flank would be immediately assailed by troops from the City, who were said to be working round into our rear." This, likewise, was a lie, but you produce one of the exaggerated effects in your original pamphlet by introducing the recreant trooper's false report as if it represented a real incident. "Some of Holkar's guns and Cavalry", you said, "were moving round to cut off the retreat."† In the text of your large book you only say, as authorised by Major Travers, "Some of Holkar's guns and Cavalry were *said* to be moving round to cut off the retreat."‡ But in your Appendix, avowedly controversial with regard to Sir John Kaye—though you leave my book to "die a natural death"—you reproduce the trooper's lie. "After Holkar's troops had begun to cut off the retreat, there was no time left to wait."§ But it is quite untrue that anyone had begun to cut off the retreat. The line of retreat on Mhow was quite open, and there was no pursuit, or menace of pursuit.

"The slow and orderly retreat from the Residency", you complain, "was denominated a 'flight'."‖ It was just its "slow and orderly character" that made it a

---

* *Evacuation of Indore*, p. 12, footnote.
† *Central India in* 1857, p. 24.
‡ P. 215.   § P. 466.   ‖ P. 226.

"flight", and showed that "the post", *i.e.*, the post of Governor-General's Agent, which could have been held, and was held so advantageously by Hungerford and Hutchinson at Mhow, "had been needlessly abandoned."

It has already been shown that neither General Travers, in his official despatch and his pamphlet of 1876, nor Sir Henry Durand, in any public or private letter, ever stated that they *saw*, or that anybody *saw*, any additional force of Holkar's troops proceeding from the City to join in the attack on the Residency. But there is a paragraph in Colonel Durand's despatch from Mhow of August 18th, 1857, which, giving you very large license on account of filial regard and respect, does in some degree extenuate the exaggerations of your pamphlet and of your large volume. It is as follows:—

"4. Considering the deliberate arrangements made by Holkar's Cavalry for cutting off European fugitives, even before a shot was fired, it was strange that the Durbar should have failed in receiving early intimation that some unusual movement was taking place. When the treacherous attack of Holkar's guns and troops which were at the Residency, was supported by additional guns and troops hurrying to the scene of action from their lines, and no word or message came from the Maharajah, there certainly was every appearance that the troops acting so unanimously must be advancing by order of the Durbar. This conclusion was natural, and at once pervaded the few troops that were loyal to the British officers that commanded them."

This paragraph really contains nothing but a reproduction of the lies devised by our mutinous Sepoys— "the few troops that were loyal"—to clear out the Residency for plunder. Major Travers, in his despatch, mentions the same "natural conclusion" on the part of his men, but obviously as a false, or at least a doubtful report, which he could neither verify by his own observation, nor confirm by authentic intelligence. Colonel Durand, having committed himself to denunciations of Holkar, based on the Sepoys' lies, from that day forward allowed the "natural conclusion" of our "loyal" troops to harden by frequent repetition into a positive statement. The statement was utterly unauthenticated, and was not merely unconfirmed, but contradicted, by all subsequent inquiries; but it suited Colonel Durand's apologetic purposes, and held its place accordingly in his irresponsible talk and in his private correspondence.

Here is another absolute, though vague, misstatement by Colonel Durand, in a matter most essential to Holkar's justification, which you cannot but know to be a misstatement, and to have been exposed in the *Last Counsels*, and which you, nevertheless, reproduce in its vaguest form, as if it were a true statement, left quite intact by your "violent and acrimonious" opponents.

On the 18th of August, 1857, a fortnight after Colonel Durand's return to Mhow, he wrote a despatch to Government which in one place you cite as "far from unfavourable"* to the Maharajah, and in another as written "in Holkar's favour."† Yet in this despatch, as you know, the best that Colonel Durand can say of the Maharajah, is that *"he may have been as ignorant of what was plotting, and as much surprised and intimidated when the attack took place,* as he represents." Everyone but yourself will, I am sure, appreciate the odious use here of the word *intimidated.* But, you say, Colonel Durand observed that "a marked distinction was to be drawn between the Maharajah and his Durbar".‡ Exactly—that is the absolute though vague misstatement by Colonel Durand that I now have in hand,—a misstatement adopted by the Calcutta Foreign Office, though contradicted by explicit details on record, and repeatedly placed before the Viceroys by your predecessors, as you now place them before the public, as genuine materials for a decision. These are the words of the despatch :—

"Whatever may be thought of the conduct of those who surrounded his person, many of whom must have known what was plotting, and some of whom were actual participators and leaders, as Saadut Khan, there can be no doubt of his Highness's anxiety to separate his own name and fame from the guilt of participation in an attack marked by equal treachery and atrocity."

Of course, if Holkar had been guilty, this anxiety

---

* P. 221.   † P. 169.   ‡ P. 221.

would have been equally manifest, so that there is nothing said in his Highness's favour so far. He goes on :—

"I have drawn a marked distinction between the Maharajah and his Durbar. Personally, he may have been as ignorant of what was plotting, and as much surprised and intimidated when the attack took place, as he represents, but this was not possible as to the members of the Durbar. Some of these were leaders in the insurrection, and many more must have been cognisant of the intrigues and tampering with the troops that was going on."

The "marked distinction" which Colonel Durand most unwarrantably drew between the Maharajah and his Durbar, was not really "favourable" to his Highness, as you try to make out,[*] but most injurious to him. Nothing could be more insidiously hostile. Anyone of ordinary common sense would say that if the Prince's daily associates and advisers had been conspiring against the British Government, in concert with our mutinous troops, he could hardly have been ignorant of what was going on. Colonel Durand, positively denouncing the Durbar, only suggests that Holkar "*may* have been ignorant". The insinuation is most unfavourable, under colour of moderation and fairness, while the denunciation of the Durbar is entirely devoid of truth.

In this letter of the 18th August, 1857, written at Mhow, while the local inquiries on which a report could be founded were in progress, Colonel Durand describes Saadut Khan as "*in his Highness's Court and about his person*", and declares that some "*members of the Durbar*" "*were leaders in the insurrection*"; the only leader whom he names being that same Saadut Khan, who was not in the Durbar, was not "in his Highness's Court and about his person", but was out of employ, and in disgrace.

The Viceregal Government eventually treated this denunciation of the Indore Durbar as if it had been, as it was, a rash and hasty denunciation, quite devoid of truth, for in reply to Sir Robert Hamilton's report, dated April 26th, 1858, founded on the local inquiries instituted, but not used, by Colonel Durand, *all* the members of the

[*] Pp. 221, 469.

Durbar, with five other officers of rank at Holkar's Court, received "the cordial thanks" of the Governor-General for their "excellent services", "loyalty", and "assistance" given to the British Government.*

The only person that Colonel Durand names as being an "actual participator and leader in the insurrection", is Saadut Khan. Saadut Khan, as you know very well, was not a member of the Durbar, and was not attached to the Maharajah's person. In your original pamphlet, *Central India in* 1857, to which the *Last Counsels* was expressly a rejoinder, you said of the insurgents, "A Durbar officer of high rank called them out to the attack," and in another passage, "One of the leaders of the insurgents was a Durbar officer named Saadut Khan, who was hanged two years ago for his share in that day's work."†

You must know now, if you did not know then, both from the details given in my book, which you leave unanswered in the hope it may "die a natural death", and from the records in your own Office, exactly what the position of Saadut Khan was. He was not an officer "of high rank". He was a Rissaldar without a Rissala,— drawing pay but having no command. He was, also, Deputy Collector of Customs, but under suspension. He was "a Durbar officer" in the same way that Captain A. is "a Queen's officer", and in no other way,—in the service of Government, but not in the Prince's household or counsels. He was a discredited person, employed in a subordinate place under Captain Fenwick, an East Indian in Holkar's service. He was a man with a grievance; and his grievance was the refusal of the Maharajah to recognise him as a member of the Durbar, as entitled to hereditary rank and emolument. When he actually became a ringleader in the conspiracy and outbreak he was a disgraced and discontented man,— disgraced by the Durbar, and discontented with the position the Durbar had assigned to him.

You do not, however, admit or notice the error

* Appendix A, The Durbar.
† *Central India in* 1857, pp. 24 and 52.

exposed by me. You content yourself with dropping the name of Saadut Khan altogether out of your book. You say nothing now about the special "officer of high rank", but employ a general insinuation that "some of his" (Holkar's) "officers were prominent among the insurgents."* None of the Maharajah's officers, except the two or three belonging to the detachment, were "prominent" or present in the outbreak. Besides the substitution of this misleading generality for the name of Saadut Khan, "an officer of high rank", you adhere to "the broad distinction to be drawn between Holkar and his Durbar."† And this "distinction" you profess to consider as "far from unfavourable" to his Highness, and as having been written "in Holkar's favour".† It was at any rate the very best thing that Colonel Durand could ever bring himself to write regarding Holkar's conduct.

Let us now see what is the very worst that, according to your newest and latest version, he ever alleged against Holkar.

Before entering on that part of my subject, I must say that in my humble judgment the "tact" of an Under-Secretary in the Indian Foreign Office who takes upon himself to malign publicly one of the most influential of Indian Princes, appears rather open to doubt. I will add, and I shall prove, that your "tact", in the private capacity of apologist for Sir Henry Durand, is very much at fault, when you bring prominently forward those dark insinuations against Holkar which your father, to all appearance, was desirous of keeping in the background. I have long searched in vain for the very worst accusation or imputation that Colonel Durand could bring against the Maharajah. I have dragged it out of you at last, and it is just what I expected,—an impalpable slander, without even an ostensible foundation. This is the very worst that you, Under-Secretary in the Foreign Office, in possession of your father's papers, and with access to all the records of the Government of India, can say against the Maharajah Holkar :—

* P. 220. † Pp. 221 and 469.

"So far as I have been able to make out from the several references to this subject scattered throughout his letters, he (Sir Henry Durand) did not consider that Holkar had actually gone against us or instigated his troops to rise. But he gradually came to the conclusion that Holkar had been trimming, and trying to stand fair with both sides, and that he had known a good deal more than he had told. 'Holkar's waiting game,' he wrote to Lord Ellenborough, 'was spoilt by the leaders of the Indore insurrection hurrying his troops and people into untimely action. He felt that their precipitation had hopelessly ruined him unless he could patch up matters with us.'"*

Here I find the strongest and most complete confirmation of all that I have written as to Sir Henry Durand's treatment of Holkar. You can only "make out" what your father's professed views in this matter were from "scattered references" in his private correspondence. In no document, public or private, in none of Sir Henry Durand's despatches, minutes, or familiar letters, can you find—any more than Sir John Kaye could—anything definite or intelligible against Holkar, or anything to verify the vague imputations and scornful calumny with which the Maharajah was continuously and confidentially persecuted by Sir Henry Durand for more than eleven years.

Let us, however, take the general purport of the "scattered references". Sir Henry Durand, having originally denounced Holkar as his treacherous assailant, "gradually came to the conclusion that Holkar had been trimming, and trying to stand fair with both sides". With "both sides"! What is meant by this? The British Government was on one side, but who was on the other in June and July, 1857? The Sepoy mutineers, and more particularly and immediately the mutineers of the Mhow brigade. The Maharajah Holkar was a highly intelligent and well-educated Prince, who had visited some of the great centres of British power in India, had made the personal acquaintance of Lord Elphinstone at Bombay, and was on terms of the closest and most cordial affection with Sir Robert Hamilton, whose children he was accustomed to call his brothers and sisters.

* P. 236.

I can anticipate the sneers with which you will greet this mention of the distinguished gentleman who carried the infant Prince in his arms to the Musnud, was virtually guardian and regent during the minority, and occupied the place of Governor-General's Agent at Indore for the long period of fourteen years. During the eight months of Sir Robert Hamilton's absence, from April to December 1857, Colonel Durand, who was acting for him, managed to blast the reputation and to blight the life of Holkar, and to produce a dilemma for himself very much like what you say Sir John Kaye propounded, viz :—"that the justification of Holkar implied" your "father's condemnation,"*—that unless Holkar was a traitor, Colonel Durand was "a bad political officer".

Sir Robert Hamilton, although the natural protector of Holkar, did not, on resuming his charge in December 1857, so much espouse the Maharajah's cause as place before Government the simple facts regarding the outbreak at Indore collected but neglected by Colonel Durand. Before leaving Indore, Sir Robert Hamilton had been authorised to read, and had read in Durbar, to Holkar, a letter from the Viceroy, Lord Canning, dated "Calcutta, 26th March 1859", announcing that his Highness was to receive a territorial reward "in due proportion" to the "Nizam and Scindia".† Until this promise, made by him as the Viceroy's representative and in the Viceroy's own words, was redeemed, Sir Robert Hamilton felt that the honour of our Government was compromised, and that his own honour was pledged to make every effort to ensure the fulfilment of that promise. You not only upbraid Sir Robert Hamilton without any apparent grounds, as "unfriendly" and "hostile" to your father, but make offensive incursions into the regions of private life, which, although they may suit your notions of "tact and firmness", appear to me hardly consistent with good manners and fair dealing. The rather ill-natured gossip about Sir Robert Hamilton's large establishment of horses, carriages, and servants, and the

---

* P. 475. † Appendix B.

marriages of his daughters, which you have extracted from Colonel Durand's private letters,* was assuredly never meant, even by him, for publication. It has no bearing whatever on the subject, except so far as it confirms a very general belief in Sir Henry Durand's habit of treating anyone who stood in his way as a personal foe and a noxious creature, and of privately denouncing him all round.

Unfortunately for Holkar, facilities for private denunciation were afforded to Colonel Durand at a very early moment, and remained constantly open to him for eleven years. Very soon after Sir Robert Hamilton had resumed charge of the Residency at Indore, on the 15th of December 1857, Colonel Durand was called "on special duty", to Lord Canning's side. From that day his private reports of what he had not seen, and of the operations in which he had not taken part, and of the Prince whom he had seen twice in three months, prevailed against the public and official statements made by the officers at Mhow who had succeeded in the work which Colonel Durand had abandoned as impracticable, and by Sir Robert Hamilton, who had been for thirteen years at Indore.

I do not hesitate to say that if he even for a time suspected Holkar, as you say he did, of "trimming with both sides", and of "playing a waiting game", that suspicion is enough to stamp Colonel Durand as "a bad political officer". It was not merely that, as Sir John Kaye justly said, he wanted "tolerance", lacked "imagination", and "could not Orientalise himself". He could not understand or appreciate, though the problem was easy enough, the personalities with which he had to deal. Holkar was, as I have said, and as no one disputes, an intelligent and well-educated Prince. He was surrounded by enlightened and English-speaking councillors, and was absolutely without any turbulent or fanatical connections. The best possible excuse for Colonel Durand having made the utterly unfounded report that "*some of those who surrounded the Maharajah's person*", and

---

* P. 198.

"*some of the Durbar*", were "*actual participators and leaders in the attack*", would be that in the three months he had passed at Indore he had, as you say, "only seen Holkar twice",* that he did not care to know who were in the Prince's confidence and intimacy, or how the Durbar was constituted. This, I say, is the best and most charitable excuse for Colonel Durand's gross misstatement regarding the Indore Durbar, but then it fixes upon him indelibly the stain you are trying to efface. The Agent who, at such a crisis, could hold aloof, in a supercilious and unsympathetic attitude, from the Prince and the Court that formed the very centre and heart of his charge, was essentially, root and branch, "a bad political officer".

You deny that your father had "an antipathy" to Holkar. You claim to have "shown" that he "wrote in Holkar's favour to Lord Canning", and that "nothing can be less inimical or indicative of the antipathy which Kaye most unjustly attributes to him than the tone of these letters".† The tone of those letters, as I have just proved, was as thoroughly inimical as their tenor was inaccurate. Not a word can be found in them that is really written "in Holkar's favour". But before coming to the "inimical" stage,—for you state that Colonel Durand "gradually" lost faith in "the Maharajah's loyalty", and that "as time went on his doubts were strengthened",‡—it is necessary to make some remarks on the Agent's intercourse with Holkar before the insurrection. You bring forward as evidence that there could be no "antipathy", the fact that Colonel Durand "had been three months at Indore, and had only seen Holkar twice". You do not perceive the true significance of that fact as evincing Colonel Durand's contempt for information and advice from Native sources, and his disregard for close and friendly relations with the Court of Indore and its notabilities. In three months Colonel Durand saw Holkar twice ; one of these visits being his formal pre-

---

* P. 474, and *Central India*, p. 69.   † P. 469.
‡ Pp. 235, 236, 469.

sentation on arrival, the other having been solicited by the Maharajah; and he never invited his Highness to visit the Residency.

On the 9th of June 1857, three weeks before the outbreak, at a conference which he specially called at the palace, Holkar warned Colonel Durand that, in the event of a mutiny at Mhow, his own troops could not be trusted, and gave the wisest advice for the emergency, that the treasure—about £130,000 in specie and £240,000 in Government paper—should not be left, as a temptation to attack, in the Residency, but should be sent off at once to the military cantonment of Mhow. The Maharajah also urged that the English ladies should immediately go to the same place, and that the Residency buildings should be made into a strong military post. Colonel Durand would not take this advice. He said that European troops were shortly expected, and that the precautions recommended would only cause alarm and tend to encourage the evil-disposed. Alarm could not be prevented. From the 9th of June to the 1st of July not only alarm was felt but frequent warnings were given to Colonel Durand. With every well-informed person expecting an outbreak, no preparations were made to meet it. He even rejected the military advice of two Engineer officers, Captains Ludlow and Cobbe—coincident and identical with that of the Maharajah—that the Residency should be entrenched, and that the treasure should be moved from a detached building into the Residency, so that there should be only one place to defend. The Uncovenanted servants complained afterwards that, although their numbers were considerable, they were not embodied or organised, and had no place of security selected into which they could retire.* The contemptible nature of the attack, when the outbreak occurred, and the ease with which a slow retirement was effected, are enough to suggest very strongly that if due preparations had been made, the results of the mutiny at Indore on the 1st

---

* Sir R. Hamilton's despatch, No. 47, of the 9th February 1858, to the Government of India.

of July 1857, might have been very different from what they were.

When we take into consideration these timely but neglected counsels, the good faith of which it is impossible to doubt, and those points as to the talents, training, and associations of Holkar and his councillors, with which Colonel Durand ought to have been familiar, his hasty suspicion and condemnation of the Maharajah and of his Durbar, are enough to convict him of being "a bad political officer". When Colonel Durand avoided the cantonment of Mhow, because he thought it would be attacked by Holkar, when he wrote to Lord Elphinstone that "Holkar's treachery was of the true Mahratta stamp",* he showed himself to be a "bad political officer".

Your contention, however, is that although, "to begin with", Colonel Durand "certainly imagined that Holkar had thrown in his lot against us", "directly Holkar disclaimed such intention, he accepted and favourably noticed the Maharajah's explanations." With the "favourable notice" I have already dealt. Then came an unfavourable stage. "He was not entirely convinced of the Maharajah's loyalty; and as time went on his doubts became strengthened."† And in another part of your book you say that your father "lost his former confidence in Holkar, and left Indore under the impression that justice would not be done". At first he had, you say, been inclined to consider him" (Holkar) "sincere in disclaiming participation with the mutineers. Nevertheless, he had felt some doubts on the subject, and they had been confirmed by one or two circumstances which occurred during the rainy season, by conversation with various natives of the country, and by the additional information which he had acquired regarding events at Indore before and during the rising."‡

This is a very remarkable passage. Although you are a barrister-at-law, and have been, I presume, a magistrate, you seem not only to be quite ignorant as to what

---

* Kaye's *Sepoy War*, vol. iii, p. 347.
† P. 469.   ‡ Pp. 235, 236.

constitutes evidence, but not to comprehend the enormity of the charge that you are making here, in your father's name, against the Maharajah Holkar. In your Appendix you say that Colonel Durand's "doubts" amounted to nothing more than this, that at the "beginning of the outbreak Holkar was playing a waiting game". And there is nothing, you urge, very dreadful in this, "considering that Sir John Kaye expresses the same doubt regarding all the Native Chiefs in India."* In the passage just quoted from the text you say that when your father left Indore he no longer considered "Holkar sincere in disclaiming participation with the mutineers", his "doubts on the subject" having "been confirmed by one or two circumstances which occurred during the rainy season, by conversation with various natives, and by additional information which he had acquired".†

Will you be so good as to tell us whether this "additional information" was communicated to the Government of India? I can find no trace or hint of it in the official proceedings.

You have now informed us that Colonel Durand, who, to begin with, inaccurately denounced "members of the Durbar" as "participators and leaders in the outbreak", and made a favourable distinction between the Maharajah and his Durbar, believed at last, likewise, in Holkar's personal "participation with the mutineers". Thus he, according to you, dropped the "marked distinction" he had made in Holkar's favour.

You endeavour, moreover, to show some cause for this change. Colonel Durand's doubts were "confirmed", you say, "by one or two circumstances", one of which you give, as follows, in a footnote :—"For example, by finding that while professing the utmost fear of their troops, the Durbar were importing a large quantity of pig-lead for musket ammunition. The lead was seized and lodged in Mhow fort."‡

You have, throughout your narrative, adopted the highly coloured and exaggerated pictures drawn by

---

* Pp. 469, 470.   † Pp. 235, 236.   ‡ Footnote, p. 235.

Colonel Durand, when he found out his mistake in having avoided Mhow, as to the unanimous misconduct of Holkar's troops. You have even improved upon them, with some little excuse from your father's loose diction, by presenting the troopers' lies about the retreat being cut off, and more guns and Cavalry approaching, as if they represented actual events that Colonel Durand had seen with his own eyes.* In the same way you grossly exaggerate Holkar's temporary loss of authority and influence during the wild excitement caused by the evacuation of the Residency. You make the most unwarrantable assertion that "Holkar was entirely powerless. He neither had nor pretended to have the smallest remnant of control when his troops rose". "He could not",† you continue, "punish or keep under restraint the leader of the attack, who came to him in his Palace, and boasted of having wounded a sahib".‡ He did restrain Saadut Khan for several hours, and that miscreant was in confinement when the Residency was evacuated, so that the mutineers were without a leader at the critical moment when Colonel Durand's little band was without defence. The consequence was that the English party was able to retire, "unmolested", "at the rate of two-and-a-half miles an hour".

You base your wild assertions as to Holkar's whole army "surging up", on an alleged statement by the Durbar Vakeel to Colonel Durand, that "the lines were empty".§ These words convey no information unless we know to what hour in the day they refer. Even in your father's own account of his conversation with Ganesh Shastri, which you vainly imagine to "set the point at rest", there is not one word to show that "the lines were empty" before Colonel Durand had retired.‖ That the Durbar Vakeel, Ganesh Shastri, who is still, I believe, living, ever said that the "lines were empty" during the attack or the retirement "at the rate of two-and-a-half miles an hour", is utterly untrue, and will not bear a minute's reflection. If any such movement of

---

* *Ante*, p. 4; *Central India in* 1857, pp. 53, 55.   † P. 464.
‡ *Ibid.*   § Pp. 215, 467.   ‖ P. 467.

Holkar's troops had taken place—nay, if a hundred horsemen had assailed them—the fugitives must have perished. It is quite true that an utter overthrow of discipline followed the news of the British officers having retired. The greed of plunder led nearly all the troops to visit the Residency in the course of the day; but some of the Durbar troops behaved very well from first to last; a certain number were accounted for as on guard at the Palace and other posts; some, including the Maharajah's Household Cavalry, obeyed the orders to remain in their quarters.

You must know—or you ought to know, with the best information at hand—that even if Holkar's troops had all behaved badly, the greater part soon returned to their allegiance and their duty. Within three days after Holkar was relieved from the pressure of our Sepoy mutineers, three columns of his troops were sent out for the rescue of British officers. And not only were several detachments of Holkar's troops constantly employed, to the end of the war, in keeping the country quiet and suppressing marauders, but they served under British officers in some of the most decisive actions against the rebels in the neighbourhood, on which occasions the Maharajah and his commanders were thanked by the Bombay and Supreme Governments.

If, then, some of the Maharajah Holkar's troops, after the terrible excitement caused by the mutiny of British troops and the flight of British officers had cooled down a little, were doing good and faithful service, it was right, I suppose, that they should be supplied with the ordinary munitions of war. I have no doubt as to the fact that Colonel Durand seized some "pig-lead", and lodged it in Mhow Fort. That at such a time he should have ostentatiously proclaimed, by many offensive and insulting words and acts, his dislike of the Maharajah Holkar, proves that he was "a bad political officer". But the circumstance you consider so important has no other significance.

You have yet another explanation of Colonel Durand's gradual belief in Holkar's " participation with the mutineers". Referring to your father's opinion as to "Holkar's waiting game", you say, "His opinion was greatly strengthened by finding that Lord Elphinstone, who had at first written strongly in favour of Holkar, was afterwards inclined to take the same view, and this upon information gained independently in the Bombay Presidency."

This is what Lord Elphinstone wrote to the Viceroy, Lord Canning :—

"Colonel Durand appears to be under the impression that Holkar had turned against us, and that he was attacked by his orders. This, however, is certainly not the case. On the same evening Holkar wrote to Colonel Durand and to me, protesting his innocence, and entreating that the march of General Woodburn's force should be hastened as much as possible."*

This is what he wrote to Colonel Durand :—

"If he (Holkar) had been ill-disposed towards us, the whole country would have risen. All the smaller Chiefs seem to have taken their cue from him; and even to the borders of Gujerat, the effects of his conduct would have been apparent. This comes to me from too many sources to admit of any doubt. Let me, therefore, beg you not to harbour any prejudices against Holkar, to whom I cannot but think we are very much indebted for the preservation of the peace in Malwa and also in Gujerat."†

You object, however, to Sir John Kaye's assertion that Lord Elphinstone, "*with all the facts before him*", pronounced in favour of Holkar's loyalty and condemned Colonel Durand's "prejudice". What, according to you, "appears from the letters quoted by Sir John Kaye", is "that very shortly after the outbreak, when Lord Elphinstone had *not* all the facts before him, he wrote to my father and others asserting Holkar's innocence".‡ I will not trouble you now to answer my big book,—let us consider that it has "died a natural death",—but should you decide on making an example of this little pamphlet and its author, perhaps you will tell us what "*all the facts*" are, and what in particular are the facts which were *not*

---

* Kaye's *Sepoy War*, vol. iii, p. 349.
† *Ibid.*, pp. 349, 350.   ‡ P. 174.

before Lord Elphinstone, when he rebuked Colonel Durand and recommended Holkar to the Viceroy's protection against that official's prejudice. You have given us your one little "circumstance" of the "pig-lead". But what are "*all the facts*"? We have under Lord Elphinstone's hand his detection and rebuke of Colonel Durand's "prejudices" against Holkar; his declaration of Holkar's good influence over "the smaller Chiefs" of Western India, "even to the borders of Gujerat"; his assurance that Holkar's valuable services in time of need "will not be forgotten by the British Government".

I think, under the circumstances, impartial readers will prefer this written testimony—consistent with all officially recorded facts—to your vague, inexplicit, and unauthenticated statements as to "personal assurances", and as to Colonel Durand "finding" that Lord Elphinstone was "afterwards inclined"* to alter his views. I cannot see that you have acquired any right or title by the scrupulous candour and accuracy of your method, to have your "scattered references" accepted without verification in preference to testimony for which I give chapter and verse.

I regret to observe that you still persist, notwithstanding my very full exposure of your error, in the presumptuous impertinence of censuring Major Hungerford, who assumed the duties of Agent to the Governor-General when Colonel Durand left the precincts of his charge. You endeavour to stigmatise Major Hungerford, whose conduct was approved and warmly commended by the Viceroy, the Commander-in-Chief, and the Commandant of Artillery, as having not been "strong before the outbreak", as having not been "ready during the outbreak", and as having been "injudicious after the outbreak". You attempt to ridicule this gallant officer, who died in 1858, as "*the Artilleryman, who, unable to stir out of Mhow, and ignorant of Holkar's conduct before the rising, established himself as representative of the Governor-General*",—for which, be it observed, he received Lord

* P. 474.

Canning's thanks,—and you take upon yourself to censure Lieutenant (now Colonel) Hutchinson as "*an equally ignorant Political Assistant, who was a fugitive under the protection of Holkar's troops*".*

In all this, it is true, you merely echo Colonel Durand, who wrote in terms of complaint and blame,—though without producing any impression on the Government of India,—regarding the Commandant of Mhow, and the two Assistants who took up his duties when he had retired to a distance of two hundred miles from Indore. "*Why Captain Hungerford assumed the powers he did*", he could "*neither understand nor approve*",—it was understood and approved by the Viceroy in Council. "*Nor*" could he "*approve that men in the position of dependence upon Holkar, like Lieutenant Hutchinson and the occupants of the Mhow Fort, should assume the political functions of the Agent*",—although nobody knew where he was, and he neither wrote to his Assistants nor answered their letters,—"*and take upon themselves to judge the conduct of Holkar and the Durbar*".

You protest against Sir John Kaye saying that Colonel Durand "had disappeared from his charge, no one seemed to know whither, and that he did not answer Hungerford's letters. This", you say, "is untrue. The force from the Residency retired at a walk, and passed Holkar's roadside posts on the march towards Bhopal. The Durbar knew perfectly well in what direction it had retired, and that my father was within the limits of his charge, for Bhopal was as much a part of his charge as Indore." You are incapable, of course, of being disingenuous, but you seem to have overlooked the fact that Colonel Durand remained less than twenty-four hours at Bhopal, the Begum having explained her inability to protect him, and that he went on at once to Hoshungabad, a British station, two hundred miles from Indore, and not within the limits of his charge.

"He was", you continue, "throughout within two days' post, and he answered all letters sent to him."†

* Pp. 222, 223, 470, 471. † P. 471.

I think not,—I think he was not, to say the least, very prompt in acknowledging the letters he received from Indore and Mhow. For more than three weeks after his retreat nothing had been heard from Colonel Durand by any of his Assistants, by Captain Hungerford, who by force of circumstances had fallen into the charge both of military and political affairs, or by the Maharajah. They had all written to him, but the Agent would not vouchsafe a reply. Although, by his own account, *"communication was easy and rapid,"** he stopped all communication for nearly a month with the English officers who were doing his work, and for more than a month with the Prince to whom he was accredited. Not a word of counsel or of encouragement came from him.

The first communication received by Holkar from Colonel Durand after the 1st of July, was an alarming letter dated Mhow, the 3rd of August 1857, containing two charges against his Highness, of having held aloof during the attack on the Residency, and of having allowed supplies and carriage to be furnished to the mutineers. The perverse and bitter spirit pervading this letter is, perhaps, most strongly exemplified by the first words in it that are intended for commendation. Colonel Durand says :—

"I have no doubt that the Right Honourable the Governor-General of India will hear with satisfaction that you avoided the disgrace which would for ever have clung to your name, had you pusillanimously given up innocent persons who had sought refuge in your Palace, to be massacred by blood-thirsty miscreants."

He cannot even be so gracious as to say, "You have done well"; he can only say, "You have not acted like a pusillanimous wretch, or a blood-thirsty miscreant."

The man who could write in such a tone, at such a time, was emphatically "a bad political officer".

I shall introduce you to some little notes—you may verify them in "the Office"—which confirm my statements on this point, not yours. Before coming to these,

---

* Despatch to Government of India, No. 207, dated Mhow, 18th August 1857.

however, I must notice your new and very preposterous complaint that the officers who performed Colonel Durand's duties efficiently and successfully during his retirement, " were endeavouring to supplant him". This is too ridiculous. Were they to run away from Mhow because he fled from Indore? Were the two Assistants, Captain Hutchinson and Captain Elliot, to strike work because the Agent had disappeared? The period of Colonel Durand's absence had been well employed by the English gentlemen at Mhow, with Holkar's help, in restoring postal and telegraphic communications, in regaining a firm hold over local resources, and in smoothing the way for military operations. The Maharajah, fortified by friendly intercourse with our officers, was able to tranquillise the country, and to spread abroad a general impression that the cause of the insurgents was doomed. If Colonel Durand's Assistants had followed their superior's example, or if Captain Hungerford had shrunk from responsibility, Holkar and his Ministers, in the absence of any British political authority, would have lost much, if not all, of their influence for good, and the rebellious faction and predatory tribes of Malwa would have gained proportionate strength.

"It would be interesting to know", you say, " what these gentlemen would have done, if while they were acquitting themselves so much to their own and Holkar's satisfaction"—and, let me add, to the Viceroy's—"the man whom they were endeavouring to supplant had let the barrier of the Nerbudda drop behind them, and allowed Woodburn to march off to Nagpore."*

Colonel Durand had no authority over General Woodburn, and no influence whatever over the march of his column. I have never understood, and I have never met anyone who did understand, what you mean by this mysterious rubbish about " the barrier of the Nerbudda".

The following sentence in a letter, dated 12th of July, from Hungerford to Durand, does not look as if "these gentlemen" were very much afraid of "the barrier of the

* P. 471.

Nerbudda being dropped", and was innocently calculated to be very galling to Colonel Durand, an Engineer officer, if he and Colonel Travers had decided—as their messenger on the 1st of July 1857, reported—on not going to Mhow, because they believed that Holkar was going to attack it.

"This fort, thanks to the hard labour of the Europeans, has been placed in such a state of defence, and we are so well provisioned, that it would take an army to attack it."

Six weeks after the receipt of this letter, Colonel Durand takes upon himself to say that, during his absence, Hungerford, Elliot, and Hutchinson had been "*in a position of dependence on Holkar*". Yet he gives no credit to Holkar, and objects to a "favourable report" being made on his Highness's "conduct".

For Colonel Durand thus continues:—

"It was, however, an object with the Durbar to anticipate, if possible, a deliberate review of its conduct, by obtaining favourable reports and opinions which might clog after-measures, and these gentlemen all fell into the trap."

"So did Lord Elphinstone then", was the marginal comment of Mr. (afterwards Sir George F.) Edmonstone, the Foreign Secretary, on this passage in Colonel Durand's despatch of the 18th of August 1857. With reference to Colonel Durand's animadversions against Captain Hungerford, Mr. Edmonstone likewise made the following marginal note:—

"The assumption of political functions by Captain Hungerford, and the manner in which he discharged those functions, have been warmly approved and commended by the Governor-General in Council. Colonel Durand did not keep these officers informed of his movements; nor, indeed, did he keep the Government informed. He left Hoshungabad about the 16th of July, and nothing was heard of him until he reappeared at Mhow. Captain Hungerford has already explained that Major Cooper ceded the command of the Mhow Fort in his favour, because Captain Hungerford was the only officer who had any troops to command. No troops were left except the European Battery."

In the same paragraph of his despatch of August 18th, 1857, Colonel Durand says :—" His Highness knows well that the Agency was never out of my charge, and that there was, therefore, no resuming of the Agency."

On this Mr. Edmonstone remarks :—" But neither Holkar nor anyone else knew what had become of Colonel Durand and his office."

Unfortunately, these notes and marginal comments, though prepared by high Ministerial officers for the aid and guidance of the Executive authorities, and often throwing much light on the progress and vicissitudes of a case, are not always forwarded home for the information of Her Majesty's Government. I shall bring a few more of them to your notice.

You urge that your father's "influence", and his alleged "prejudices" and "misrepresentations", could not " have kept Holkar out of his due"; that the Maharajah had "a steady advocate in Sir Robert Hamilton, and had perfectly impartial judges. Lord Canning, Lord Lawrence, and Lord Mayo, during my father's life", you continue, " Lord Northbrook and Lord Lytton, after his death, and the various Secretaries of State concerned, were surely capable of forming an opinion for themselves."*

Certainly they were, if the proper materials for "forming an opinion" had ever been placed before them. But, as I shall show, " the Office" has ruled the Empire ; "the Service" has conspired against an impartial judgment. In the words of Sir John Kaye, "Holkar has been sacrificed to the justification of Durand."† A vague denunciation of Holkar was convenient as a screen for Colonel Durand's failure and flight. Colonel Durand had committed himself, by his declarations and his movements, to a prejudiced view of Holkar's conduct. He had reported that he was "attacked by Holkar", and that " Holkar's treachery was of the true Mahratta stamp". Under that suspicion he had left the precincts of his charge at the critical moment, and had, in particular, kept away from the military station at Mhow, where he

* P. 470. † *Sepoy War*, vol. iii, p. 346.

would have been quite safe and at his post. Subsequent inquiries, instituted by himself, entirely negatived every suspicion against Holkar. He could not justify these unfounded suspicions, or the false movement into which they had misled him. But he never distinctly renounced them. On the contrary, he came back to them again and again, in every form but that of a formal report, or of an intelligible accusation. He kept up the bad impression by his personal presence and influence in high office for eleven years, and it was carried on and heightened by his colleagues and successors. Rules and principles of Executive procedure have been set aside, and records have been misrepresented, with no better motive than private and professional sympathy. The result is that a Prince of the Indian Empire, who did good service in time of need, is branded with a false charge of cowardice and treachery—for that is what it amounts to—without the foundation of any official report or statement, in defiance of the only official report on his conduct that ever was made, by the suppression of existing evidence, and the suggestion of evidence that has never existed.

Two Secretaries of State, one of whom is now in the Cabinet—Lord Derby and Lord Halifax—have in vain issued instructions and expressed wishes in favour of justice being done to this injured and slandered Prince. The Viceroys and the Secretaries of State have been unable to contend against departmental earwigging, and the misuse of records in Calcutta.

The Indian Foreign Secretary is, as you say, "the responsible adviser and right hand of the Viceroy". Upon him and his Assistants devolves the important duty of collecting and laying before the Viceroy and his Councillors all the papers bearing on each case awaiting decision, usually with an "Office-note", summarising its history, and frequently submitting an opinion on the merits, and some suggestion for a settlement. I shall show that with regard to the conduct and services of the Maharajah Holkar in 1857 this duty was not performed in good faith by the Political Department, but was perverted for the exculpation of Sir Henry Durand, and that thus the Viceroys and Secretaries of State were prevented from "forming an opinion for themselves". Very naturally relying on the guidance of their Ministerial subordinates, they were led to overlook the fact that all the formal documents of the time bore witness to the Maharajah Holkar's fidelity and active help, and that there was no official report or statement on record condemnatory of his Highness's conduct on any particular day or in any particular incident. The permanent officers of the Calcutta Foreign Department offered certain gratuitous and obscure expressions of dislike and ill-will against the Maharajah Holkar, which seem to have been taken as if they were founded on some adverse report or statement against his Highness, written at the period in question. No such document exists.

I shall show that in 1870, the occasion demanding something more than these obscure expressions of dislike, a hostile statement was at last presented by Mr. (now Sir Charles) Aitchison, sufficiently definite in its purport, but without any foundation or verification of an official nature,—contradicted, in fact, by documents which Mr. Aitchison did not bring forward.

It is by the suppression of the truth as officially reported, and the suggestion of false matter or malignant fancy in conversation, private correspondence, and secret "Office-notes", that Holkar has been "kept out of his due", and our statesmen kept in the dark. I make no complaint of official routine. Ordinary routine has been set aside and violated throughout these proceedings. The distinguishing peculiarity of Holkar's case is, that if any Viceroy or Secretary of State, dissatisfied with vague imputations and hints of "awkward revelations" in reserve, were to call for any official report condemning Holkar's conduct on the 1st of July 1857, it could not be produced, for no such official report exists. There is nothing definite or intelligible on official record against the Maharajah Holkar. He has been publicly condemned and deprived of his promised reward on the strength of secret hints and surmises; and whenever one of these involves an allegation of fact, a very brief and simple inquiry invariably proves that allegation to be untrue.

When it seemed, from the lapse of time, that you had no intention of answering my book, published in 1877, I began to hope that I had done with you and with Sir Henry Durand. Even when the advocate's duty, the just cause and the strong case, are all equally clear, the task of refutation, exposure, and detraction cannot be agreeable. You have compelled me to resume it most unwillingly by your unjustifiable charge against me of having published " a tissue of untruth". And though the task is rendered imperative by your book, it is not rendered more congenial to my nature. I must not dwell on the subject, but I may be allowed simply to claim for myself, even in your estimation, those homely human feelings that can honour filial reverence for a personality in which there was assuredly much to be admired and much to be loved. Nor have I, let me assure you, been able to read unmoved the details of that sad and strange fatality which ended a distinguished and laborious career at a moment of hardly earned success, or of the still more sad and affecting fatality that may well have made your father think for ever after of " Mhow and Indore" with " the same feelings" of " burning, because suppressed, indignation" and of " boiling wrath".*

I wish I could say no more. But my ungracious duty must be fulfilled. There is nothing, then, in your book to dispel, and much to confirm, the impression of Colonel Durand's character commonly entertained by his contemporaries, that he was a man with whom, to use a colloquialism, it was "difficult to get on",—a *mauvais coucheur*,—a man who was intolerant of his neighbours' objects and opinions when they diverged from his own, and who was morbidly over-conscious of his own merits and claims. The numerous passages in your book tending to confirm that impression may be said to culminate in that extraordinary sentence written by him in 1864 :—

* See pp. 227, 228, 291.

" Bare justice is not what I have had meted out to me through life. I speak of man, not God."*

At least, it may be said, he drew the line somewhere in his protest against the want of appreciation in high places. If he did not bear his crosses and his losses as patiently as Job, he did not go quite so far in his complaints against the powers that be as Job's wife suggested.

He did not get on well with Lord Lawrence when the latter was Viceroy. Lord Lawrence writes as follows to the Secretary of State, in a letter dated March 13, 1868 :—

"I may say with perfect truth that I was instrumental in Sir Henry Durand getting his seat in Council. Nevertheless, ever since he entered it, I have had difficulties in managing matters with him. He is so unbending, so acrimonious, that it is hard to work with him."

Lord Lawrence's biographer, forming his judgment not only from the documents at his disposal, but also, as he says, from "conversations with other members of the Council, and high officials who were best acquainted with all the circumstances", pronounces Sir Henry Durand to have displayed habitually "a highly impracticable temper in public matters", and when in Council to have "acted as though he were inclined to oppose every measure which did not originate with himself."†

But he was not in Council when Lord Lawrence arrived in India in 1864. He was then Secretary to Government in the Foreign and Political Department, and in that capacity, as you tell us, he got on badly with the Viceroy. And one great cause of their difference was, you inform us, the style and character of Colonel Durand's "Office-notes". That is a very curious and interesting fact in connection with the matter in hand, because "Office-notes", prepared and submitted at each stage of the proceedings by the gentleman who for the time being

* P. 315.
† *Life of Lord Lawrence*, by R. Bosworth Smith, M.A. (Smith, Elder, and Co., 1883), vol. ii, p. 534.

was "the right hand of the Viceroy", have been, as I shall prove—and as you are well aware—the chief engines for Holkar's confusion. The differences with regard to these "Office-notes" rose to such a height, you say, that at last the Governor-General issued orders "that all Foreign Office work should be submitted to him without note or opinion".* Whether the first Office-note of the series I shall cite, written by Colonel Durand and dated the 4th of August 1864, was one of those to which Lord Lawrence objected, I have no means of knowing, but it will strike most people, I think, as being well calculated to call forth such a prohibition. You can look at the original in the Office, and satisfy yourself on this point, and on the accuracy of my citation.†

Sir John Lawrence, Viceroy of India, sends a memorandum to the Foreign Office on the 1st of August 1864, stating that the Secretary of State, Sir Charles Wood (now Viscount Halifax) has written, under date 4th July, requesting that he "will take care that Holkar receives certain advantages in reward for his conduct during the Mutiny, as promised to him by Lord Canning", and he calls for "the particular papers which bear on this point". Colonel Durand, Foreign Secretary, desired that they should be previously sent to him by Mr. Aitchison, the Under Secretary, with a note. Mr. Aitchison's note, dated 3rd August 1864, embodied a statement as to alleged liberal concessions and compensations that had been granted to Holkar, and ended by saying that there was no trace in the Foreign Office records "that Sir Robert Hamilton was ever instructed to make any promise to Holkar at all". Lord Lawrence remarks on this :—

"But Lord Canning must have written to Sir Robert Hamilton demi-officially, for Sir Charles Wood tells me, as a matter beyond all doubt, that a promise was made and communicated in open Durbar."

One of the concessions to Holkar mentioned in Mr. Aitchison's note was the repayment of the expense of

* P. 321.   † Appendix C, The Secret Papers.

troops raised by his Highness during the rebellion to replace our mutinied Contingents—no reward or "donation", of course—and it is to this that Colonel Durand alludes in the following note, which also accompanied the papers :—

"I refer to my note of the 6th of December 1863, from which it will be seen that the three lakhs' charge made by Holkar was ridiculous, and that the Governor-General made him a pure donation when his Excellency allowed that sum to be paid to Holkar. The latter has got, therefore, all that Lord Canning thought he should get. He was, also, given the Star of India—why, no one could ever make out—and it deteriorated the value of the decoration in the eyes of those who, like the Begum of Bhopal, knew Holkar's conduct.
4-8-64.   "H. M. DURAND."

Here we find Colonel Durand appealing to a bad opinion of Holkar entertained by the Begum of Bhopal. You have already brought him before us declaring that Lord Elphinstone eventually gave up the good opinion of Holkar, which, in his Lordship's recorded words, "had come from too many sources to admit of any doubt".[*] This "Office-note" is thus extremely remarkable in itself, and worthy of our attention at present, both with reference to the occasion that called it forth, and to the occasion that has compelled me to come forward.

Colonel Durand, in 1864, wishing to cry down Holkar as a false and recreant Prince, cannot "make out" why the Star of India was conferred on his Highness by Her Majesty the Queen. In 1884, you, with the same object, now become essential as an apology for your father's procedure, cannot "make out" why the "territorial reward", assigned to Holkar by Her Majesty's Government and by the Viceroy, has been refused and is withheld. You acknowledge at last, what no one had ever previously been able to extract, that Colonel Durand unofficially and secretly set down Holkar as "a participator with the mutineers", but you cannot "make out" why he did so. With all your "scattered references" you cannot "make out" what your father meant. You

[*] *Ante*, p. 25.

do your very best. You call Mr. Dickinson "a pamphleteer"; you suggest that all who have defended Holkar are either "paid agitators" or "ignorant enthusiasts". Although, you say, it would have been "easy" to answer my book, you "do not attempt it". Instead of the "refutation" of "a string of misstatements", which, you say, would have been "easy", you offer the very characteristic story about the "pig-lead", and the very questionable invocation of Lord Elphinstone. That is all that you can "make out" in 1883.

And all that Colonel Durand could "make out" in 1864 was that Holkar ought not to have had the Star of India, and that the Begum of Bhopal "knew Holkar's conduct". As to what Lord Elphinstone knew, you are quite silent. Colonel Durand was equally silent as to what the Begum of Bhopal knew.

These are notable specimens of the "tact, firmness, and judicial aptitude"[*] which you, no doubt, assume to be hereditary and inherent in the Calcutta Foreign Office. For my part, I am quite confident that to all impartial readers a very distinct impression of the weakness, even to nullity, of Colonel Durand's imputations, and of the strength of his rancour against Holkar, will be given by the tenor and temper of the brief note in which the Calcutta Secretary even goes out of his way to impugn the grant of honours by Her Majesty—a matter quite beyond his province. With what political or judicial propriety, in what logical connection, was the name of the Begum of Bhopal invoked to point a sarcasm against Holkar? Even if she could have been called upon for her testimony, in place of that which Colonel Durand had never supplied, or for her opinion, in support of Colonel Durand's solitary prejudice, what could she have known in July 1857, 100 miles off, more than was known by the British officers at Mhow? It must be remembered that on the 9th of July, when Colonel Durand was writing to Bombay and Calcutta that Holkar's *"treachery"* was *"palpable"*, and *"of the true Mahratta stamp"*, Holkar had already been for four days in close intercourse and active co-operation

[*] Pp. 280, 281.

with the Commandant of Mhow, and three columns of the Maharajah's troops were out in concert with our officers. In all probability Colonel Durand was merely recalling to mind in 1864 something that he had told the Begum of Bhopal himself in 1857 during the perturbation of his flying visit, and not anything that could possibly have come within the Begum's own cognisance. This is, in all probability, the sole basis of the assumption that Lord Elphinstone's opinion was altered. Colonel Durand privately gave free expression to his loose guesses as to Holkar's "waiting game", and Lord Elphinstone, who was a man of exquisite courtesy, did not rudely put him down. The strange invocation of the Begum of Bhopal, as a witness or a judge, by the Foreign Secretary to the Government of India, passed, likewise, without the animadversion it deserved in the Council Chamber at Calcutta, and was, unfortunately, never forwarded to London. The adverse opinions already recorded were once more sent, in reply to Sir Charles Wood's requisition, accompanied by Mr. Aitchison's unfavourable report, but, under Sir John Lawrence's direction, *without* Colonel Durand's note. If Sir Charles Wood had seen that note he could hardly have failed to detect its weakness, its malice, and its impropriety.

But I am really not sure that the eccentric note of the 4th of August 1864, is the worst specimen from your Office that I have to produce.

The mystery of Lord Canning's and Lord Lawrence's refusal to do justice to Holkar is almost entirely cleared up by the personal presence and influence of Colonel Durand for eleven years, from 1859 to 1870. The assumption of his local and immediate knowledge supplied every deficiency in the records, and superseded everything that conflicted with his irregular imputations. But in July 1870 there were great grounds of hope that Holkar's claim would receive impartial consideration. Sir Henry Durand was no longer present at head-quarters. He had been appointed Lieutenant-Governor of the Punjaub. The Viceroy, Lord Mayo, well disposed after a personal interview with his Highness, promptly repelled an attempt by the permanent officials to reject or impede the Maharajah's appeal on a point of etiquette or form. Mr. Aitchison, the assistant and successor of Colonel Durand at the Calcutta Foreign Office, happened, also, to be temporarily absent at the commencement of the proceedings of 1870. These favourable conditions were, however, made of no effect, just as the Viceregal Government was on the verge of perceiving the truth, by the personal intervention of Mr. Aitchison, immediately on his return.

In 1864, Colonel Durand, unable to produce any testimony or official statement describing Holkar's misconduct, invokes the Begum of Bhopal as a witness or a judge of something he does not specify.

In 1870, Mr. Aitchison, equally unable to produce any testimony or official statement, gives for the first time a description of Holkar's misconduct as if it had come from official records, but really in flagrant contradiction to authentic records which might have been, but were not, produced.

In the absence of Mr. Aitchison, Mr. LePoer Wynne, his Assistant, had stumbled over the strange fact that Colonel Durand had promised to report on "the conduct of Holkar and his troops"; and although Mr. LePoer Wynne was assured in the Calcutta Foreign Office that "no such paper had ever been received", "much search" was made, under his directions, and he announces "a renewed search", these "missing papers" being most "*important as illustrating the reasons which induced Lord Canning and Lord Lawrence to refuse a territorial reward*".

It was time for some one better acquainted than Mr. LePoer Wynne with all the previous incidents to stop this critical inquiry, which, if pushed on too far, must have disclosed the fact that there was nothing on record as to any misconduct on the part of Holkar or the Durbar. There was nothing to "illustrate" the previous adverse conclusions but vague rumours, and the menacing promise of a report, which was "missing". The total deficiency of "reasons" as to Holkar's forfeiture struck Mr. LePoer Wynne as a very remarkable point.

Mr. Aitchison came back at this crisis. He knew, of course, that no papers were missing, but in his supplementary "Office-note" he does not refer to Mr. LePoer Wynne's bootless research. He does not mention Colonel Durand's name. Mr. (now Sir Charles) Aitchison can alone explain whence he extracted the stuff which he laid before the Viceroy in Council as the evidence, and the "reasons" which Mr. LePoer Wynne declared to be wanting. He quotes no despatch; he names no informant; but, by a direct accusation against the Maharajah Holkar of coquetting with treason for four days, he covers up the bare place which Mr. LePoer Wynne had so inconveniently displayed. Here are Mr. Aitchison's own words in a note dated 5th August 1870 :—

"There is this difference between Holkar and those Chiefs who have received territorial rewards, that *Holkar did not, like them, at the first burst of the mutiny, take that open and decided part with us that he ought to have done. The attack upon the Indore Residency occurred on the 1st July*, 1857. *It was not till the 5th that he took any decided steps to show with which cause he intended to throw in his lot.*"

Mr. Aitchison makes a charge against Holkar of having wavered and hesitated for four days. Now he proceeds to explain how base the motives were under which that hesitation at last came to an end.

"*During these four days our position at Mhow had been rendered secure by the vigorous measures adopted by Captain Hungerford. There was no longer any doubt as to the strength of our position. Accordingly*, on the 5th of July, the bodies of the slain were buried by Holkar's order, *and the Maharajah on that date, and not before, sent a deputation to Mhow to express his regret at what had occurred.* I think, *therefore*, that Lord Canning took a thoroughly just view of the Maharajah's services when, in his despatch, No. 6, of 18th January, 1860, he wrote," quoting the passage in full, that Holkar's "conduct" was unworthy of "either respect or gratitude".

These, in short, are the "reasons", hitherto "missing", "which induced Lord Canning and Lord Lawrence to refuse a territorial reward". Colonel Durand's declamatory prejudices, detected and rebuked by Lord Elphinstone at Bombay, had struck deep root in the official circle at Calcutta. Here we have them reproduced by Mr. Aitchison, when pressed for evidence and reasons, in the form of definite and injurious charges against Holkar. What was Mr. Aitchison's authority for the inaccurate story with which he misled Lord Mayo? Whether he received it as scripture or as tradition, its inaccuracy is manifest and indisputable.

Mr. Aitchison says that "*Holkar did not, at the first burst of the mutiny, take an open and decided part with us*", and that "*Holkar took no decided steps to show with which cause he intended to throw in his lot*" until the 5th of July. He says that "this is the difference between Holkar and those Chiefs who have received territorial rewards": and the despatch consequent on these proceedings, points to this as the "clear and broad distinction between the case of Holkar on one side, and those of Scindia and of the Begum of Bhopal on the other". But there was no real ground for any unfavourable distinction between the conduct of Holkar "at the first burst of the mutiny", and that of Scindia and the Begum of Bhopal; or if there was any distinction, it was entirely in favour of Holkar. There was no more truth in the distinction between Holkar and Scindia, than there was in the distinction, which you vainly imagine to have been meant as favourable to Holkar, between the Maharajah and his Durbar.

In briefly referring to the difficulties which assailed the rulers of Gwalior and Bhopal in the great convulsive crisis of 1857, and of the temporising expedients to which they had to resort, there is no wish to detract from their great services. I am deprecating, not instituting, an invidious comparison.

When, on the mutiny breaking out at Gwalior, the Resident, Colonel Macpherson, sought refuge at the Palace, Scindia declared that, in consequence of the feeling of his troops, "he could not protect" him "for an hour". The Resident therefore left Gwalior for Agra.* When Colonel Durand, in his retreat from Indore, arrived

* *Return to the Lords* (77 of 1860), *Honours and Rewards*, pp. 102, 103.

at Sehore, the capital of Bhopal, the Begum expressed her inability to shelter him or any English officer at her capital, or in her dominions. Colonel Durand, therefore, instantly left Bhopal, and made for the British cantonment of Hoshungabad.

For fully four months, from the 14th of June to the 15th of October 1857, Scindia was only able to restrain the mutineers of the Gwalior Contingent—in the words of Colonel Macpherson, the Political Agent—by donations of pay, and " by the delusion that he must at length place himself at the head of the rebels".* Holkar was not compelled to carry temporising expedients to such an extremity. He was not reduced to disguise his adherence to the British cause for a day, or for an hour. On the very day of the outbreak he openly resisted it. On the very day of the first outburst of the mutinies at Indore and Mhow, Holkar did noble service. Although he could not communicate with the Governor-General's Agent during the terrible hour and a half that preceded his retreat, the Maharajah apprehended the leader of the outbreak and kept him in charge during the most dangerous crisis; he sent back to the scene of bloodshed and confusion the misguided leader of his detachment, with orders that must have damped the ardour of all who feared or hoped anything from their own Prince; he stopped any reinforcement of the mutineers and rabble engaged in attacking the Residency; checked the concourse that would otherwise have flocked there with irresistible effect, and prevented the pursuit of Colonel Durand. It is almost certain that by remaining close to his Palace, keeping as tight a hold as was possible for some time over the bulk of his troops, he did much more good than if he had started for the Residency in the midst of an infuriate crowd, ignorant of his real intentions, but bent on mischief themselves.

Holkar, moreover, on the very day of the outbreak, and in the words of Sir Robert Hamilton, "at the risk of his own life", saved within his Palace the lives of a number of Europeans, East Indian and Christian subjects

* *Return to the Lords* (77 of 1860), *Honours and Rewards*, p. 107.

of the Queen. On that very day he sent a deputation to the British authorities at Mhow, and sent off letters to Colonel Durand and to Lord Elphinstone, the Governor of Bombay.

Mr. Aitchison says that on the 1st of July 1857, Holkar did not " take an open and decided part with us"; that " it was not till the 5th that he took any decided steps to show with which cause he intended to throw in his lot"; and that "on that date, and not before, he sent a deputation to Mhow". But there were then within Mr. Aitchison's reach despatches proving that Holkar had sent a deputation to Mhow on the 1st of July, the day of the outbreak, and that he had never hesitated or ceased for an hour to take an open and decided part on our side.*

This new indictment was, nevertheless, quite enough for Lord Mayo, when he was assured by Mr. Aitchison that it had sufficed for Lord Canning. "For my own part", says Lord Mayo, "I am quite satisfied with the description given in the Secretary's note of Holkar's actions at the time of the mutiny." That description, with the accompanying inferences and surmises, was not only unsupported by the records at Mr. Aitchison's disposal, but was contradicted by them.

The adverse decision was, in due course, conveyed in the form of a letter to the Governor-General's Agent at Indore, dated 10th November 1870, in which the Maharajah is told again that although graciously "overlooked", in consideration of the services he "subsequently rendered", his conduct on the day of the outbreak not having been worthy of "either the respect or the gratitude of the British Government", necessitated "a clear and broad distinction" between his case and those of Scindia and the Begum of Bhopal, and "invalidated" his claim "to an acknowledgment of his services by the extension of his territory".

In the same letter, the Maharajah is, moreover, told that he has received certain "pecuniary concessions" and "substantial marks of favour", which constitute "a

* Appendix D, " The Deputation to Mhow".

cordial appreciation" of his services, and a sufficient reward for them. Even if it could be shown that the transactions detailed in the despatch were exclusively beneficial to Holkar, which he denies, the argument would still be quite irrelevant. The question is not of incidental concessions or courtesies or compliments, but of a condemnatory sentence, and of a promised reward withheld on account of it.

It became the duty of Major-General Sir Henry Daly, Agent to the Governor-General, to communicate the contents of this despatch to the Maharajah, and to leave him a copy of it. In the conversation which ensued, as narrated by Sir Henry Daly, in a despatch dated "Indore Residency, 21st November 1870", his Highness, "speaking quietly and calmly", said: "I see Lord Mayo can do nothing for me, that nothing can be done in India, therefore I must press my case in every possible way in England." In order to dissuade him from taking this course, the Agent urged upon Holkar that it would be most imprudent for him to brave an open discussion or to court publicity. In Sir Henry Daly's own words, "*I endeavoured to impress upon his Highness the pain which would certainly fall upon him by dragging to light events which the Government of India will willingly let sleep, that the British officers who were in the Residency at Indore on the 1st of July are still living, and that should he force an inquiry, the evidence of the Natives, too, would tend to prove on that day, at any rate, the Maharajah had not chosen our part.*"

It is obvious, from Sir Henry Daly's silence on that point, that the Maharajah showed no apprehension as to the publication which Sir Henry Daly "endeavoured to impress upon" him "would certainly" cause him "pain". The Maharajah made no objection to "events being dragged to light". Sir Henry Daly, in short, completely failed in "impressing upon his Highness", as he had wished, the imprudence of "forcing an inquiry". He totally failed, likewise, in creating any alarm in his Highness's mind at the prospect of the despatch of the 10th of November 1870, being published, "*for public information"—" in order that the merits of the case might be generally understood".* Sir Henry Daly is a very distinguished soldier; and the Government of India may have had better material for estimating his diplomatic and judicial capacity than this one instance of an offensive exhortation, aimed point blank at a Prince in person, and quite missing its mark. It is worthy of notice that Sir Henry Daly having completely failed in his object, seems to have been incapable of appreciating or even perceiving the significance of his failure. What his failure really meant was that no evidence, British or Native, against Holkar, had ever existed.

Mr. Aitchison, in an "Office-note" sent round with Sir Henry Daly's despatch, thinks that "for the present it would be very improper to publish the papers, but if Holkar begins to agitate, Colonel Daly's proposal is not a bad one". Holkar, Mr. Aitchison also says, "will act very foolishly if he begins to agitate his case at home, and *will force Government to make awkward revelations of his conduct during the first four days after the outbreak at Indore.*"

The combined assurance of these two high functionaries must have only tended still more to the satisfaction of a Viceroy in Council already contented with Mr. Aitchison's "description of Holkar's actions". It made such an impression upon one Councillor, Sir Richard Temple, that he at once minuted as follows:—"*If Holkar 'tries it on', and gets his 'face blackened' in consequence, his Highness will have himself to thank.*"

And yet there was not then, and there is not now, any such evidence as that which Sir Henry Daly conjured up in vain for the intimidation of Holkar. There were not then, and there are not now, any "*awkward revelations*" held in reserve, which could "blacken Holkar's face". You have not been able "to make out" anything, with all your "scattered references".

If any hostile evidence had been recorded or attainable, if any "*awkward revelations*" had really been kept in the background, some hint of them must have come out in the course of these proceedings. But there is no such hint or trace. Every deliberate report, everything that is in official form and order, is favourable to Holkar. Everything that is against him is vague in sense, and irregular in form. When Colonel Durand was driven to say something in 1864, he could only express his feelings by a mysterious invocation of the Begum of Bhopal, and an indiscreet impeachment of Her Majesty's prerogative. When Mr. Aitchison was closely pressed in 1870 on account of "the missing papers", he could not cite anything official, but had to draw his condemnatory "description of Holkar's actions" from some private or personal source without a name.

The case, as now presented, is a very simple one. It is narrowed to the direct citation of two living persons, Sir Charles Aitchison, Lieutenant-Governor of the Punjaub, and General Sir Henry Daly, who resides in this country. The judgment of independent politicians, and even of Ministers, has always been on the side of the injured and insulted Prince; but officialism supports its professional colleague, statesmanship is baffled and defied, and a Prince's honour is sacrificed to an Agent's credit. On the other side, there was until 1870 only one accuser —an accuser who brought no charge—Colonel Durand. For eleven years the disgrace and deprivation of the Maharajah Holkar depended on the inexplicit vilifications, secretly reiterated in 1864, of Colonel Durand, and on his almost constant presence. So the matter stood until 1870. From that year Sir Charles Aitchison and Sir Henry Daly are morally responsible. On the "description of Holkar's actions" by Sir Charles Aitchison, also secretly recorded, the decision of 1870 is expressly grounded,—that being the only adverse decision in which any grounds of judgment have ever been set forth.

Until Mr. Aitchison's "description of Holkar's actions", there was not on record, even in secret, one distinct or intelligible word explaining what was the Maharajah's misconduct "at the time of the mutiny" which had rendered him unworthy of "either respect or gratitude", and created the "broad distinction" in favour of the Begum of Bhopal and Scindia. In his "Office-note" of the 5th of August 1870, Mr. Aitchison gives the much required and missing word, quite distinct and intelligible, but quite unwarranted. This "description of Holkar's actions" satisfied Lord Mayo, because he naturally assumed that it was drawn from official records. It was not. It was unauthenticated even as an accusation. It was quite new, and quite untrue.

At the same crisis, when the redress of a great wrong was within reach of Lord Mayo, Sir Henry Daly, by alleging that there was "evidence", both European and Native, of Holkar's misconduct, confirmed the unfounded statement by which Sir Charles Aitchison had "satisfied" the Viceroy.

These two living accusers have rejected a personal challenge to justify or withdraw their accusations, which I felt bound to offer for their acceptance. It is natural and easy for them, with all their advantages of position and prescription, to revile and ridicule my mission. I certainly have no power to force an answer from them. Evidently I have no power to extort an answer from you. My book was so sure "to die a natural death" that you would not refute it, although the task would have been, you think, an easy one. You may now flatter yourself, and may be flattered in the narrow circle of Chowringhee or Simla, into the belief that this Letter demands no more attention, because you could, if you chose, refute it likewise. But in the much larger circle I address, and where I shall be heard, the vapouring evasions of your class will not avail you.

It will not avail to say that the acts of Sir Charles Aitchison and of Sir Henry Daly have obtained the approval and confirmation of the Government of India. That superior sanction, as I have shown, was wrongfully obtained. In their unjustifiable treatment of the Maharajah Holkar's appeal, those two gentlemen must have been actuated and biassed—almost unconsciously, I believe—by considerations and motives neither judicial nor political, but private, personal, and professional. In common charity I am driven to refer to the prevailing

Anglo-Indian prejudices of race and class, because I see no milder method of accounting for Mr. Aitchison's unwarrantable "description of Holkar's actions on the day of the meeting", or for Sir Henry Daly's equally unwarrantable declaration as to "evidence" of the Maharajah's misconduct.

Sir Henry Daly and Sir Charles Aitchison, and a great many Anglo-Indian officials, like yourself, probably had, and have now, a feeling that the unretracted bad word of a British dignitary like Sir Henry Durand is as good as evidence against a Mahratta Prince, and ought to counterbalance all opposing testimony. But you, as a barrister-at-law, ought to know that this is a very serious error. It is, likewise, more than probable that in Anglo-Indian official circles, at home and abroad, a feeling would prevail that a highly placed member of the Civil or Military Service is, from every point of view, a person of far greater consequence, of more importance and value to the Empire, than any Nawab or Rajah. But this, also, is a very great mistake. The truth is not to be rejected because the Ministerial officer who, under some strange misconception, put it aside, and put something else in its place in 1870, is now the Lieutenant-Governor of the Punjaub. Lieutenant-Governors come and go. The House of Holkar is firmly rooted in the soil, and is an invaluable factor in the conservative equilibrium of India. Were it just, it would not be politic to outrage and disregard the permanent realities of the Empire, in order to uphold an error, or to screen from discredit for a time the mere accident of a day and a Department.

The supply of officials, even of Secretaries, Political Agents, and Lieutenant-Governors, quite up to the average standard, is constant and practically unlimited. But Princes of the Empire, though easily destroyed or disheartened, cannot be made and cannot be replaced, either by patronage or by competitive examination.

The Indian Principalities, the self-governed provinces, are, and always have been, not accidental, but essential, constituents of British power in India. Our Indian

Empire would never have come into being, and cannot continue to flourish or to exist, without them. Without Native allies, Great Britain could not have won her way to virtual supremacy between 1756 and 1819. Without the aid and influence of the Indian Princes, the mutinies of 1857 would have swelled into a general rebellion, so tremendous that the restoration of British rule could only have taken place at an incalculable cost, and with horrible and ruinous results of devastation and disorganisation.

The mere existence of the Princes, irrespective of their active aid or countenance on our side, prevented the rebels from getting leaders of weight and capacity, and from obtaining anything like a political centre or even a belligerent status. The Nizam's authority was invaluable in the Deccan, and was more or less of a restraint over Mohammedan fanaticism in every part of India. The good effect produced by the combined support of Holkar and Scindia throughout Hindostan and Malwa can hardly be over-estimated. But during the most critical months of 1857 and 1858, when the provinces round Delhi and Lucknow were in full revolt, Holkar stood alone in Malwa and Central India; for Scindia was a fugitive—his Durbar and army had "gone", and he was only able to return to Gwalior in June 1858, escorted by British troops. The influence of Holkar was, also, pre-eminent among the Mahrattas of Western India. "All the smaller Chiefs", said Lord Elphinstone, "seem to take their cue from him." In a remarkable article which appeared in the *Quarterly Review* for July 1858, well known to have been from the pen of Mr. (now the Right Honourable Sir Henry) Layard, who had lately returned from a tour through India, while the rebellion was at its height, the writer attributes "the maintenance of our rule in India to the fidelity of the Nizam of the Deccan, Scindia, Holkar, and the Rajah of Putteeala", and adds: "The Presidency of Bombay has been saved only by the energy, foresight, and judgment of Lord Elphinstone, although its army was on the eve of revolt, and its population, especially that of the Mahratta country, ready for insurrection."*

As to the condition of Central India, take the following extract of a letter from Sir John Lawrence to Lord Stanley :—

"June 16, 1858.

"Gwalior has fallen into the hands of the mutineers, with, I fear, a couple of millions of treasure. Unless we can retake it, which is at least problematical, a general insurrection throughout the Mahratta States may be anticipated. Central India is a strong country, difficult for military operations; and, with plenty of money, soldiers can be procured in any numbers."†

This gives force and strong confirmation to the following passage in Sir Robert Hamilton's letter of the 26th of April 1858,—the only official report on the conduct of Holkar and his Durbar in 1857 that was ever made :—

"What has really foiled them has been the personal fidelity of Holkar, Scindia, and Baiza Baee. Had any one of these declared for the Peishwa, our difficulties would have been beyond conception; the smaller thakoors and rural chiefs would have instantly joined the standard of their sovereign; every village would have been openly hostile."‡

And here is a similar extract from one of Earl Canning's published despatches :—

"There is no doubt that if the Mahratta plots in the West had not, by active operations on a comparatively small scale, been nipped in the bud, the great body of rebels in the East—that is, in Central India, Bundelcund, and near the Jumna—would have acquired much greater strength for resistance on a large scale."§

You can, confessedly, "make out" nothing against these historical facts with your "scattered references", nor can they be nullified either by Colonel Durand's equivocal sneer of 1864, or by Mr. Aitchison's novel figment of 1870. As you have nothing else to offer, I cannot doubt that from your disclosures alone, without

* *Quarterly Review*, July 1858, p. 265.
† *Life of Lord Lawrence*, by R. Bosworth Smith (Smith, Elder, and Co.), vol. ii, p. 302.
‡ *Return to the Lords* (77 of 1860), p. 116.
§ Military Letter from the Viceroy in Council to the Secretary of State, dated 4th April 1861, No. 45.—*Papers*, 498 of 1863, p. 5.

the aid of my comments and my additional revelations, impartial readers will begin to have grave misgivings as to the "tact and firmness", the "sympathy with the feelings of rulers and people", the integrity and the public spirit, with which the work of the Foreign and Political Department is carried on—the chief place in which, you say, "is regarded as the blue riband of the Civil Service", "an almost certain stepping-stone to the highest posts in the Empire".

God help the Empire, when those who have stepped into its highest posts are possessed by such "tact" and such "firmness", such "sympathy with rulers and people", such "judicial aptitude", and such public spirit, as have been displayed by Sir Henry Durand, Sir Charles Aitchison, and yourself, in your dealings with our "loyal, steadfast, and faithful ally",* the Maharajah Tookajee Rao Holkar.

But you have yet another specific offence, in addition to the "pig-lead" affair, to lay to the charge of the Maharajah Holkar. "Not many years ago", you say, "the Governor-General was forced to return one of his memorials as containing remarks regarding my father and Lord Canning, which were positively intolerable."† Yes, the Governor-General was "forced". That is the very word. Lord Northbrook, *who had then been about a week at Calcutta*, was misled by Mr. Aitchison, his "right hand", and keeper of the papers, as completely as Lord Mayo had been, by the very safe and convenient device of not allowing him to see the papers at all. Redress was refused to Holkar in 1872 by the absolute rejection of his memorial, without hearing or consideration, on the ground of his having "presumed to write of the Governor-General's Agent, Sir Henry Durand, and even of the late Viceroy, Lord Canning, in highly unbecoming and objectionable terms". Leaving out of consideration its evasive character and object, this is a plea quite peculiar to Anglo-Indian officialism. It seems to me to be very feeble and very unjudicial.

* *Return to the Lords* (77 of 1860), p. 119.
† P. 462.

If it should be urged that the reputation and credit of the late Sir Henry Durand are more precious than those of Sir Robert Hamilton, who is living, or that more faith ought to be placed in the infallibility of the late Lord Canning than in the judgment of the present Earl of Derby or of Viscount Halifax, I can only say that all these considerations appear to me to be wide of the mark. Respect ought certainly to be paid to the memory and reputation of the dead, but not at the expense and to the dishonour of the living, or at the risk of public mischief. This is a question of truth and justice, and of great political import, not one of personal deference or forbearance. For example, Holkar is living. The unjustified maintenance of this calumny is not merely an injury to that Prince, his House and State, but is an unpurged and unrebuked offence against the Imperial Crown and the British Government of India. This is preeminently a case in which it may be said, *Nullum tempus occurrit Regi.* There can be no term of limitation for the redress of a calumny which has misled the Viceroy, and frustrated the declared intentions of Her Majesty's Government.

Sir Henry Durand, who hastily denounced and persistently maligned Holkar, is dead. Lord Elphinstone, who eulogised Holkar, and warned Sir Henry Durand "not to harbour prejudices" against the Maharajah, is also dead. Sir Henry Durand, who was then living, was mentioned, it is said, in Holkar's memorial of 1870, "in highly unbecoming and objectionable terms". On the other hand, Sir Robert Hamilton, who, in the only official despatch on the subject, described Holkar's conduct on the 1st of July 1857, as admirable, and who traced the ultimate safety of British power in Central India to the personal fidelity of Holkar, is mentioned by the Ministerial subordinates of the Indian Foreign Office in terms that are beyond a doubt "highly unbecoming and objectionable". He is put down as a "notorious advocate" of Holkar "at home", whose "mischievous advocacy" is quite undeserving of credit. You have done all that bad taste and a bad case could prompt, to improve on this unprovoked insolence.

Sir Robert Hamilton is living, surrounded by children and grandchildren, and neither to him nor to them, it may be presumed, can his reputation be a matter of indifference.

You seem, by-the-by, to attach great importance to the fact, communicated to your father by Sir John Kaye, that the latter was "an intimate personal friend" of Sir Robert Hamilton. I was misled by the "my dear Sir" style of one or two notes I came across among Mr. Dickinson's papers into forming a different opinion, and expressed it hastily and, I regret to say, somewhat rudely, not in the book which has escaped " severe treatment" at your hands *because* you consider it "violent and acrimonious",* but in an unpublished paper, which you have probably seen. I owe an apology to you for this error—the only one of any description that you have helped me to correct—but the point itself is utterly insignificant. Sir John Kaye's careful impartiality is quite unimpeachable; while the positive, as well as the weightier negative, evidence of prejudice and calumny is drawn from Colonel Durand's own papers, not from anything that Sir Robert Hamilton could have supplied. The error of judgment that Kaye imputes to Colonel Durand in evacuating the Residency (absurdly exaggerated by you into the imputation of "an act of poltroonery"†) is, as you very justly observe, an "entirely separate matter" from Colonel Durand's "treatment of Holkar",‡ the real matter at issue. But, as you consider the question of intimacy to be important, I may as well mention that I have never seen Sir Robert Hamilton. When I was preparing the *Last Counsels* for the press I applied to him for information as to one or two facts ; but, during the last seven years, I have had no correspondence or communication with him, or with any member of his family. It is not, therefore, as a personal friend, but simply as one who has always upheld those views of the position of the allied and protected States in the Indian Empire, upon which there was a substantial agreement between Sir John Kaye, Mr. Dickinson, and

* P. 476.   † P. 475.   ‡ P. 464.

Sir Robert Hamilton, that I undertake to defend the last-named gentleman from your reiterated suggestion that he was very wrong, and was deservedly censured by the Government of Lord Ellenborough for "the unauthorised elevation of young Tookajee Holkar" to the musnud of Indore. Sir Robert Hamilton, as you may see from his despatch to Lord Canning's Government of 1st February 1859,* has never acknowledged any error in this case. He was entirely in the right, and Lord Ellenborough's advisers were entirely in the wrong. The Government of India was saved by him for the time, and in a most momentous instance, from drifting into that stream of sham precedent, sham prerogative, and flagrant prevarication, which carried Lord Dalhousie into the disastrous policy of breaking up the Empire and constructing new departments. Sir Robert Hamilton was so well informed as to the law, custom, and precedents really applicable to Hindu successions, that he never suspected the perverse and grasping heresy propounded at Calcutta, until he found himself censured for not having fallen into it.

But you gentlemen of "the blue riband and stepping-stone" department, in defiance of statesmanlike instructions from home, in the face of Viceregal and departmental recantations, are perpetually relapsing into that same heresy—the heresy that sanctifies the extinction of allied States and the growth of salaried Commissions.

I have had good occasion to watch the sayings and doings of the Calcutta Foreign Office; and I declare that not one of those distinguished persons who have occupied the place of what you call "the right hand of the Viceroy" during the last twenty-five years, has ever been able to stick to a consistent principle on the subject of succession and annexation for a single year, or even through a single despatch. When the practical temptation of aggrandisement and patronage presents itself before the departmental mind, precept and principle give way at once.

You say that Sir Henry Durand was "decidedly op-

* *Return to the Lords* (77 of 1860), pp. 121, 123.

posed to the sweeping annexations of Lord Dalhousie, which, while they weakened our military position, had also unsettled the minds of our Indian feudatories, and sown fear and distrust broadcast".* Yet with reference to the only two actual cases that were proposed while he was at the head of the Foreign Office—those of Dhar and Mysore, most iniquitous and impolitic both of them —he was bitterly bent on annexation.

The retrogressive heresy that you accept as doctrine would cover a complete recurrence to the "sweeping annexations" of the Dalhousie reign of terror. "It would be extremely interesting," you say, "in face of all that has been talked and written by ignorant enthusiasts or paid agitators in England, to work out this question. There is hardly a great Native State in India which has not, strictly speaking, lapsed to the Crown; and under any other Government but that of England the majority of these States would long ago have been absorbed. By the English Government their existence has been artificially prolonged." This is totally erroneous, and exhibits complete ignorance on your part of the International law, the Indian law, and the Indian history, bearing on the question. It is totally untrue, and without the least political or historical foundation, that "the great Principalities of Gwalior, Indore, Jeypoor, and Baroda" have "lapsed to the Crown", or that "under any other Government but that of England these States would have been absorbed".†

The whole question of adoption, and of confirmation and investiture, has been so fully argued, and the iniquity of Lord Dalhousie's doctrine of "lapse" so thoroughly and unanswerably exposed by Mr. J. M. Ludlow,‡ and by myself,§ that I will only bring to your notice the candid

---

* P. 282.   † P. 286.

‡ *Thoughts on the Policy of the Crown towards India* (Ridgway, 1859).

§ *Retrospects and Prospects of Indian Policy* (Trübner, 1868), pp. 10 to 26. See also an excellent pamphlet on "Adoption", by a distinguished gentleman now at Calcutta, the Hon. Vishwanath Narayun Mandlik, member of the Legislative Council, published in London by Smith, Elder, and Co. in 1866. Mr. Robert Knight, editor of the *Statesman*, has also exhausted the subject, from every point of view, with reference to estates as well as States.

confession of the Indian Government in Lord Canning's Adoption Despatch of April 30th, 1860, which contains (paragraphs 17, 19) the following passages :—

"We have not shown, so far as I can find, a single instance in which adoption by a Sovereign Prince has been invalidated by a refusal of assent by a Paramount Power."

"There is no example of any Hindoo State, whether in Rajpootana or elsewhere, lapsing to the Paramount Power, by reason of that Power withholding its assent to an adoption."

You say that the "connection" of the reigning Princes of Indore and Gwalior "with the former ruling family"—begging the question audaciously with that word "*former*"—"is very slight". You are quite mistaken. The present Maharajah Holkar of Indore is first cousin, the present Maharajah Scindia of Gwalior is "nearest in blood",* to his immediate predecessor. Both of them are descended in the male line from the common ancestor of *all* their predecessors. What more could you say, what more could you expect in any Royal family—our own, for example—of Europe or Asia?

But I am wandering from my real object, already, I think, fully attained, that of clearing myself from the charge, which you do not attempt or "propose" to justify, of having published "a tissue of untruth". I really had not any intention, when I began this Letter, of carrying the war so far into the enemy's camp. I certainly had no intention, and have none, of denouncing your method as not being in harmony with the utterances and the style of those who have stood of late years at "the right hand of the Viceroy", and into whose place you may very naturally aspire to step in your turn. On the contrary, both your pamphlet and your book strike me as eminently characteristic of your department, and quite in keeping with the tone and manner of the very best official society in Calcutta. You say that you were "much tempted" to answer my book.† Well, you resisted the temptation, but you succumbed to another, far more excusable in your case than in that of Sir Charles Aitchi-

* *Succession by Adoption of Princes in India* (50 of 1850), pp. 37 and 88.   † P. 476.

son, and one of the besetting temptations of the class to which you belong. You thought more of the narrow circle in which you move, and of its petty maxims, than of the broad bounds of the Empire, and of the great principles on which its peace and stability depend. You thought more of the personal credit of your father—and here is the great excuse for you, and for you only—than of what you would, perhaps, call abstract justice. You have been relying too much on the dignity and security of Anglo-Indian officialism, on your big salaries and your sky-blue ribands. These things count for a great deal with Anglo-Indian functionaries and their parasites, but for very little with Imperial statesmen, or with intelligent citizens of the Empire, when once they are roused —no easy matter, I confess—to look into anything Indian.

You think that Mr. Dickinson's posthumous work will "die a natural death", and that more people will read your book than have "ever heard of Mr. Dickinson or his pamphlets".* It is possible that the establishment of "The John Dickinson Association" in London, and the names on its first Committee, may very soon convince you that here, also, you have made a great mistake.

You appear to imagine, in common with most of your official compeers, that the suggestion of an advocate being *paid*, is enough to destroy all the effect of his advocacy. "The cap fits!" Yes—you are quite right. I apply your indirect sarcasm, as you wished your readers to apply it, directly to myself. I am a half-pay officer, with no private means worth mentioning, and my large expenditure in advocating the redress of many Indian wrongs and the adoption of a liberal and truly Imperial policy, during the last twenty years,—with substantial and, as I believe, beneficial results,—has not come entirely from my own resources. I have done much unpaid work, and have seen myself in print much too often at my own cost. I am under the guidance and control of no one. But it has been very satisfactory to myself, and not devoid, I believe, of public advantage, when I

* P. 476.

have been able to combine literary and political work, and to obtain material aid from a publisher, or a client, or a fellow-worker. All that I claim is that my work has been conscientiously taken up and conscientiously performed. I have never accepted the position of advocate in a cause which I did not conceive to be at once just and capable of some settlement, and to have in it no element of hostility or mischief to the Empire. I have always aimed at scrupulous accuracy and moderation in all my statements and in all my arguments. I have, to the best of my judgment and ability, done my work well.

I have too often had to complain,—and never more often than with reference to the case now before us,—that the gentlemen of your department, although very handsomely paid, do their work badly. In the year 1870, Mr. Aitchison, "the right hand of the Viceroy", was receiving a salary of £4,000 a year. When he evolved from his inner consciousness the inaccurate statement that Holkar had played "a waiting game" for four days,* in contradiction to the records in his keeping, and thus misled Lord Mayo, I think he did his work badly. Judging by the standard I have set up for myself, it appears to me that in the month of August 1870 Mr. Aitchison's work was badly done, and his large salary not fairly earned.

If there is, indeed, no power in the Empire to redress the wrongs done in your Office and to improve the quality of its work in general, then my humble efforts as a critic and an advocate are entirely thrown away. But I do not yet despair of the commonwealth. There are latent forces in the Crown and in the constituencies that may wake us all up before long, and save the Empire from the selfish and stifling pressure of "the Office" and "the Service".

I have Sir, the honour to be,
Your most obedient servant,
EVANS BELL.

* *Ante*, pp. 41 to 44, and Appendix D.

APPENDIX.

A.

THE DURBAR.

(Page 14.)

The persons who formed the Durbar or Council at Indore, and with whom alone the Maharajah was in the habit of consulting in affairs of State, were (1) his own brother, Kashee Rao Holkar (K.C.S.I.); (2) his preceptor and Private Secretary, Oomed Singh; (3) the acting Dewan, Ramchunder Rao Bhao; (4) Bukhshee Khoman Singh, the Maharajah's fellow-student, Commandant of Cavalry (C.S.I.); (5) and Gunput Rao Seetaram, commonly called Gunesh Shastree, the Durbar Wakeel, or agent for daily communications with the British Resident. These five were all good English scholars, and during the two days of rebel ascendancy at Indore—2nd and 3rd July—actually became as much the objects of the mutineers' hate and fury as if they had been Europeans. Besides these there were (6) Bhowanee Singh Sir-nobut, head of the Household Horse; (7) Bhim-gir, head of police; and (8) Ram Rao Narain, the hereditary and titular Dewan. During Colonel Durand's retirement, their own observations and experience, and their inquiries at Mhow and Indore, convinced Major Hungerford and Captains Hutchinson and Elliott, as certified, for example, by Major Hungerford in a letter to Rao Oomed Singh, the Maharajah's Preceptor and Councillor, dated "Mhow, February 1st, 1858", that "the whole of the members of the Indore Durbar, during the time of the disturbances of the city, vied with the Maharajah in displaying feelings of unflinching loyalty and devotion to the British Government, even at a time when such feelings exposed them to great danger from a mutinous soldiery". All of the above-named members of the Durbar, with five other officers of rank at Holkar's Court, received "the cordial thanks" of the Governor-General for their "excellent services", "loyalty", and "assistance" given to the British Government [*Lords' Return* (77 of 1860), *Honours and Rewards*, pp. 119, 120, 125].

It may be said in extenuation of Colonel Durand's hasty suspicion and denunciation of the Indore Durbar, that he can have known little of the character and qualifications of any of these gentlemen, with the exception of Gunput Rao Seetaram, the Durbar Wakeel, who afterwards accompanied him in the field and received a specific reward from our Government, for during the three months of his residence at Indore, he had only seen the Maharajah himself twice.

B.

LETTER OF THE VICEROY, EARL CANNING, TO SIR ROBERT HAMILTON, BART., K.C.B.

Which was read by the British Agent in the Indore Durbar.

(*Page* 17.)

"Calcutta, March 26, 1859.

"DEAR SIR ROBERT,—This letter will catch you at Bombay, and I am sincerely sorry to think that it is the last which I shall address to you in India. Your departure is a great loss to the Government, and I only hope that it may be a proportionate gain to yourself in recruited strength and health.

"I had not much hope that the news which I telegraphed to you from the India House would detain you, and am not surprised at your decision.

"I wish that the rewards to Scindia and Holkar and the Nizam could have been settled before your departure, though with the latter you have nothing to do directly. It will require a strong influence to make all of them contented, and a new Governor-General's Agent will be at a disadvantage in this respect. There is not much difficulty about the Nizam. The difficulty is to reward Scindia and Holkar in due proportion to the Nizam without disturbing our Customs Line to an extent which we cannot afford, and without making over to their rule populations which have long been under ours. But the problem is nearly approaching to a solution, though not one which satisfies me.

"I do not see much difficulty about the Contingents; but we shall have to spend more money upon them.

"I have not been able to find your Memorandum upon military operations, respecting which you wrote some time ago. It was with me at Allahabad when I first went there, and possibly the Commander-in-Chief may have it. I have asked him, and will send it after you when I get hold of it.

"Do you think that there would be any gain in dividing the Central India Agency into two Agencies? This has been suggested, on the ground that the one is more than a single officer can properly manage. So far as regards having a chief officer at Scindia's Court, as well as at Holkar's, instead of a subordinate officer as at present, I like the proposal. The working of the Gwalior business through Indore is, on urgent matters, a serious disadvantage; but in other respects I see no gain in it. Of course, the salary of each reduced Agency would be below that of Indore as it stands. Indeed, this will be diminished in the case of your successor, irrespectively of any division of duties.

"I have not forgotten your heavy losses in 1857; but your compensation must stand or fall with that of others. You have, I hope, a good chance of recovering a considerable portion.

"Good-bye, my dear Sir Robert, and once more accept my sincerest thanks for your indefatigable and valuable aid. I have received none that has been given with a more hearty willingness, I well know; and therefore there has been none which it has been more agreeable to me to accept.

"Believe me, etc.,

"(Signed) CANNING.

"There is a farewell despatch from the Governor-General in Council still to go to you.

"To Sir R. Hamilton, Bart. "(Signed) C."

C.

THE SECRET PAPERS.

(Page 36.)

The following note from Mr. John Dickinson's pen, evidently intended to have been inserted somewhere in that "Protest and Rejoinder" on behalf of the Maharajah Holkar which he did not live to finish, is necessary as a partial explanation of his access to records that are not usually brought to light.

"I must observe, as I shall have to quote a number of 'secret' papers in the course of my argument, that there was nothing dishonourable in the way these papers came into my possession, and therefore there is nothing dishonourable in my using them. I have always been perfectly frank and aboveboard in my dealings with the Government, whether friendly or hostile. I have defended them at my own cost and peril in cases where I thought they were right—as, for example, in their sharp struggle with the Indigo Planters, and in the matter of Her Majesty's assumption of the Imperial title,—and I have attacked them in the most public manner when they seemed to me to have been in error; so that when I attack, if the gates of the fort are opened to me by friends within, it is legitimate warfare for me to take advantage of it. When copies of documents which demonstrate the injustice with which Holkar has been treated, are freely given to me by a third party, I should be doing a great wrong to Holkar if I suppressed them."

The "secret" documents constitute in themselves a history of Holkar's remonstrance, and of the manner in which the Government of India was, on each successive occasion misinformed and misled. Copies of them have been placed in the British Museum and in the London Library.

D.

(Page 45.)

DEPUTATION TO MHOW ON THE NIGHT OF 1st JULY 1857.

Extract of Letter from Captain Hungerford to the Brigade Major, Saugor, No. 422, dated Mhow, Fortified Square, 2nd July 1857.

"6. At 9 p.m. last night, it was reported that an agent from Holkar had arrived to communicate with Colonel Platt, and had been stopped by the cavalry piquet stationed on the Indore Road."

The officer with the picquet was Major McMullen, afterwards Cantonment Magistrate at Mhow.

I have said (p. 45) that Mr. (now Sir Charles) Aitchison ought to have known that the Maharajah Holkar sent a deputation to Mhow on the very day of the outbreak, and that he did not wait till the 5th of July. Here is the proof of it.

No. 4207.

To Sir ROBERT N. C. HAMILTON, Bart., Agent G.-G. for Central India. Foreign Department.

"SIR,—I am directed by the Governor-General in Council to forward for your information the accompanying copy of a letter from Captain T. Hungerford, Commanding Bengal Artillery, Mhow, dated 19 ultimo, No. 460, in which favourable mention is made of Gunnesh Seetaram Shastree, the Sudder Vakeel at Mhow of the Maharajah of Indore.

"I have, etc.,
"(Signed)   G. F. EDMONSTONE,
"Secretary to the Government of India.
"Fort William, 13th October 1857."

No. 460.

To the Secretary to the Government of India, dated Mhow, 19th September 1857.

"SIR,—In my Report to your address I omitted to mention the services of Gunnesh Seetaram Shastree, the Sudder Vakeel at Mhow, on the part of H.H. the Maharajah of Indore.

"Almost all communications with the Durbar passed through the hands of the Vakeel, and I am much indebted to him for delivering them faithfully and promptly. On the night of the 1st July he came over to Mhow from Indore for the purpose of reporting what had occurred at Indore to the Officer Commanding the station, but unfortunately was stopped by a picquet on the Indore road, and the communications he then wished to make were not received. The Europeans saved at Indore when the massacre occurred received much kindness and attention at the hands of the Vakeel, and when they could be safely brought to Mhow, were conducted to the Fort by the Vakeel.

"The Maharajah will doubtless duly appreciate the services of his servant, but I beg to bring his services to the notice of Government, in the hope that, as he exerted himself ably and faithfully to aid communication between the Durbar and myself, the Government may be pleased to encourage an officer who has fulfilled his duties so well.

"(Signed) T. HUNGERFORD,
"Captain,
"Commanding Bengal Artillery, Mhow."

"True Copy.
"(Signed) W. R. SHAKESPEAR,
"Officiating 1st Assistant Agent G.-G. for C. I."

"Docket No. 765.
"Forwarded to Gunnesh Seetaram Shastree Vakeel for information by desire of Officiating Agent G.-G. for C. I. [Colonel H. M. Durand.]
"(Signed) W. R. SHAKESPEAR,
"Officiating 1st Assistant A. G.-G. for C. India.
"Indore Residency, Camp Mhow, 30th Octr. 1857."

Sir Robert Hamilton was then in Political charge with the Field Force under Sir Hugh Rose (Lord Strathnairn), and did not arrive at Indore until December 15th. The letter from the Government of India with its enclosure was consequently delivered to the Officiating Agent, Col. H. M. Durand. Thus it is certain that Colonel Durand was fully aware of the fact that on the night of the outbreak on the 1st of July 1857, Holkar sent a deputation to Mhow.

www.ingramcontent.com/pod-product-compliance
Lightning Source LLC
Chambersburg PA
CBHW030351170426
43202CB00010B/1336